Second Edition
Beat Estate Tax Forever

Planning for Future Generations

Protect the Family Business,
the Farm,
your Lifetime's Labors

Michael Gilfix, Esq.

Palo Alto, California
Nationally known author, speaker, practitioner, certified specialist

Gilfix & La Poll Associates, LLP
2300 Geng Road, Suite 200
Palo Alto, California 94303
Toll Free 1(800) 244-9424
1(650) 493-8070
www.Gilfix.com

Table of Contents

Dedication

I dedicate this book to Myra Gerson Gilfix, whose advice, support, and insights are a constant source of clarity and inspiration.

Acknowledgments

Particularly when a book is time sensitive, help from others is essential. Fortunately, I had the help I needed. Ashleigh Alcock took over publication and many other responsibilities. Her help was absolutely critical. Mark Gerson Gilfix contributed to my thinking about "multi-generational planning."

I received excellent and timely substantive suggestions from tax attorney Francis A. La Poll and Myra Gerson Gilfix. They also provided assistance with editing, as did Jamie Arielle Gerson Gilfix.

My friend and Stanford Law School classmate Jeffrey Yablon annually publishes a wonderful book, <u>As Certain as Death: Quotations about Taxes</u>. I liberally borrowed quotes contained in his book. I also borrowed many words of Len Tillem, a remarkably insightful radio show host in California's Northern Bay Area.

Insurance professional Jack Bellevue helped me with insurance illustrations. Don Maruska, my good friend and business coach, offered practical and important guidance about the best approach to maximize success at every level. Many of my friends and colleagues, too many to name here, helped craft an effective title for this book and added extremely useful advice about its circulation and impact. Sincere thanks to all of them.

I thank and acknowledge you, the reader, for sharing this book with others and ensuring its broad distribution.

Finally, I thank our excellent staff at Gilfix & La Poll Associates for ongoing patience and commitment to quality services for our client community.

Disclaimer

This book is presented solely for educational purposes. The author is not offering it as a legal or other professional services advice. Every individual is different and the advice and strategies contained herein may not be suitable for your situation. You should seek the services of a competent professional before implementing a plan to address estate or other tax exposure. Examples are fictional. Any likeness to actual persons, either living or dead, is strictly coincidental.

Preface: Why This Book is Vitally Important for You and Your Family

Most of us don't like to think about the two great inevitabilities: *death and taxes*. Yet, that is what this book is about: the planning you can do to protect virtually all of your assets from the punishing estate tax.

The first edition of this book was written in and for 2012 because the level of estate tax protection was expected to drop to only $1 million on January 1, 2013. That didn't happen. The surprise to all of us was the extension of the $5 million estate and gift tax protection. I am therefore compelled to update and substantially rewrite this book in light of this overriding development.

I worked very hard to make this book understandable. The use of some "legalese," however, is inevitable. This is why I include a Glossary and a list of Acronyms that define many of the terms that are used in this book. Refer to it often.

Also for the sake of simplicity and understanding, I sometimes refer to the "$5 million" exemption or planning opportunity. This figure is used in the text and many examples because it is a simple, round figure. It makes some examples easier to understand.

In fact, the level of gift and estate tax protection is actually $5,250,000 in 2013. This amount will increase annually, as it is indexed for inflation.

This means that you can actually pass along – by gift or at death – a minimum of $5,250,000 this year. Even if you transferred $5 million by gift in 2011 or 2012 to "lock in" that protection, you now have another $250,000 that you can protect for your family – if you are so fortunate to have a large estate.

Yet, this book is particularly for you if your estate is over $3 million. If your estate is under that amount even though the sophisticated estate tax avoidance techniques will not play a role in your planning, the explanation of "fundamentals" and dynasty trusts will be indispensable. You don't have to have a $5 million estate to benefit from this book and from tax planning opportunities. Why? There are at least three reasons.

First, your estate could grow to the point where estate tax exposure becomes a reality. If you take sophisticated planning steps now, your estate can be completely protected.

Second, the law could change. There are many members of Congress who believe that the current level of protection is too high. They would reduce it to perhaps $2 million or $3.5 million. Anything can happen.

Third, and perhaps most importantly, the use of "dynasty trusts" will protect assets you leave your children and grandchildren from estate tax exposure when they die. For example, you may leave your son $2 million worth of assets. If he invests it well, it could easily exceed $5 million by the time of his passing. If he has his own assets – assets he earns and grows during his lifetime – in addition to what you leave him in a properly drafted dynasty trust, his total estate could easily exceed $5 million. Inflation alone suggests that the $2 million you leave him could be worth over $10 million after thirty years of growth.

If your estate exceeds $3 million, you must plan carefully to avoid tax and otherwise address your family's needs or your estate will suffer. You must assume that your estate will grow or that legislation will change to create estate tax exposure.

Finally, and although I explain most of the planning options that are available to you, I made no effort to identify every option and every variation. Time, space, and good judgment place limits on how many details can realistically be absorbed.

Tax and estate planning is a complicated process. While a good fiction writer abhors giving away a story's conclusion in an introduction, I revel in giving it away: **You need to act, to work with an experienced estate and tax attorney to help you win the tax planning challenge.**

Contact our office, Gilfix and La Poll Associates, LLP of Palo Alto, California, at www.gilfix.com for professional assistance or more information.

"The primary goal of estate planning is not the avoidance of tax. The primary goal is to assure you of a wonderful quality of life. Tax avoidance and asset protection objectives must be harmonized with this overriding objective." – M.G.

Chapter 1: 2012 and Beyond – An Unprecedented Year of Opportunity

"The $5 Million Tax Break" -- Wall Street Journal, January 29, 2011

The estate tax is a rapacious tax. It taxes assets on which you have already been taxed. While you earned it, you paid income tax. When you sold it, you paid capital gains tax. At the time of your death, the estate tax steps in and takes thousands, hundreds of thousands, or even millions of dollars away from your family.

Because of an aversion to estate tax, countless people acted in 2012. They took advantage of a remarkable opportunity. They transferred $5 million or more to the next generation –

$10 million or more for couples – without paying tax[1] because it appeared that the level of protection was about to plummet to only $1 million per person as of January 1, 2013.

This was the first time in American tax history that an individual could give away a minimum of $5 million without paying any gift tax. Previously, the cap on the amount of gifting that could be achieved without exposure to gift tax was only $1 million. This opportunity was and remains particularly powerful because of low asset values, low interest rates, and "valuation discounts" that are currently available.

This opportunity was expected to disappear in 2013 when the level of gift and estate tax protection was scheduled to drop to $1 million. To make it even worse, the effective level of estate tax was to increase from 35% to as high as 60%.

Instead, as a welcome surprise, Congress extended the $5 million level of gift and estate tax protection into 2013 and beyond.[2]

---

[1] This became the law when the Tax Relief, Unemployment Insurance Reauthorization, and Job Creation Act of 2010 was passed by Congress and signed by the President on December 17, 2010.
[2] American Taxpayer Relief Act of 2012, signed into law on January 1, 2013.

CHART A

Estate and Gift Tax Protection
2012 and 2013 Comparison[1]

2012	2013 and Beyond
Estate Tax Exemption: $5,120,000	Estate Tax Exemption: $5,250,000
Gift Tax Exemption: $5,120,000	Gift Tax Exemption: $5,250,000
Estate Tax and Gift Tax Rate: up to 35%	Estate Tax and Gift Tax Rate: 40%

So, you have a choice. You can make significant gifts over $10 million for a married couple - to be certain that assets are transferred without exposure to the punishing estate tax upon your death. Alternatively, you can retain ownership of your assets, plan creatively and protectively, and rely on increasing levels of estate tax protection upon your passing.

The idea of giving your assets is challenging. It is never easy. It runs counter to many of our instincts. But if doing so could save your family a fortune, should it not be considered?

---

[1]American Taxpayer Relief Act of 2012, signed into law on January 1, 2013.

What is it really about?

The most obvious objective is to plan to avoid or minimize tax and to protect your assets for your family. More significantly, the real goal is to plan for the health, success, and fulfillment of your progeny. This can be complicated. This can be fun.

It may involve the creation of a family retreat to be certain that family members will convene at least annually into the indefinite future. It may involve the creation of a family foundation or a Family Mission Statement. See Chapter 10 for a discussion of family values, avoiding "trust babies," and related topics.

"I worked all my life to build what I have. I'll be damned if I'll let it all go out the window on my death."
– B.T., a client of the Gilfix & La Poll office

Chapter 2: What Is In Your Taxable "Estate?" What Will be Taxed at 40%?

A. What Is Included

Surprise! It includes everything you own, and perhaps more.

Let's be clear about what is in your estate. It may be more than you think.

Most obviously, assets titled in your name or in your revocable trust, are yours and are included in your taxable estate.

Perhaps less obviously, the following are also included:

• IRAs, 401(k)s, and other retirement accounts.

• The life insurance "death benefit" if you own it, pay premiums, or have any control over it.

• Accounts you funded and over which you

serve as "custodian." These might be accounts you set up for your children or grandchildren and into which you have made $14,000 "annual exclusion" gifts.

- Assets in your name or in your revocable trust.

- Trust assets that are not yours, but where you have a "general power of appointment." You have this power if you can decide where the assets pass on your death. You may be given this power by others and be unaware of it.

- Assets you are likely to inherit from a parent or others. Include life insurance policies and IRA and other retirement accounts where you are the designated beneficiary.

- Life insurance policies you give to others during the three years immediately preceding your death.

- Life insurance policies where you have "incidents of ownership."

- Real property in which a "life estate" is held.

- Assets which you gave away, but retained the power to revoke the transfer or a "power of appointment" or "reversionary interest." Yes, very technical!

- Annuities in your name.

- Real property held in joint tenancy.

- Joint bank accounts (funded with your money).

- Bank accounts or other financial instruments that are in your name and titled "payable on death" (POD) or that "transfer on death" (TOD) are usually included in the taxable estate.

This list is not comprehensive. Other assets can sneak into your estate because of arcane tax laws that are designed to – guess what – increase your tax liability.

* * *

B. Estimating Your Estate

Here is a worksheet that will let you figure out the size of your taxable estate.

Hint: do not "lowball" the value of your home and other real property. At the time of your passing, an objective appraisal determines the value of real property. Be realistic and, if anything, optimistic about the values.

CHART B: VALUING YOUR ESTATE

Residence (less mortgage)	$_____
Total additional Real Property, less mortgages	$_____
Total Stock, Bonds, Cash, etc.	$_____
Total IRAs & Retirement plans	$_____
Total Life Insurance (death benefit amounts)	$_____
LLC, S or C Corporations, LLP, FLP interests	$_____
Total Business Interests (less debts)	$_____
Expected Inheritances	$_____
TOTAL ESTIMATED ESTATE	$_____

Surprised at how large your estate is? The fact is that most of us have estates larger than we would have guessed or estimated.

* * *

C. What is "Wealth?"

There is no agreement about what it means to be a wealthy person. To many, the "millionaire" designation is the obvious definition of wealth. To others, particularly where real property values have increased significantly, the focus may be on $1 million worth of liquid assets in addition to a residence and retirement assets.

> *The vast majority of individuals with larger estates define wealth as "double whatever I have."*

A number of studies have explored this question. Individuals with at least $1 million worth of liquid assets or individuals with incomes in excess of $200,000 or individuals with overall estates valued at no less than $3 million have be queried on the question of what it means to be wealthy.

Only one relatively clear answer emerges from these inquiries. The vast majority of individuals with larger estates define wealth as "double whatever I have."

This is an insight worth noting. It means that a person with a $4 million estate is not likely to see herself as wealthy. It means that a person with a $500,000 estate will view an individual with a $2 million estate as being wealthy. It has profound sociological and political significance. It also underscores the need for an objective, professional review of your estate to be certain that appropriate tax planning steps are taken. Do not, in other words, forgo sophisticated planning because you feel that you are not wealthy. Acknowledge what you have. Plan accordingly.

Chapter 3: The Estate Tax and Gift Tax – How Do They Fit Together?

A. Estate Tax

The estate tax came into being nearly 100 years ago, and the gift tax followed shortly thereafter. The exemption amount started at $50,000 in 1916, remained relatively steady until 1977 when it jumped to $120,000, and has been increasing ever since. The maximum estate tax rate started at 10%, but by 1935 it had increased to 70%, hitting 77% for the years 1941 to 1976. The rate started declining in 1982, and is currently at 40%. Despite its variation, and notwithstanding its elimination for one year (2010), the estate tax is a permanent fixture in our approach to taxation and intergenerational transfers of assets.

A selective history of the estate tax – since 1990 – illustrates the relative volatility of this tax. Its relative unpredictability underscores both the difficulty of planning and the need for planning. As "Chart C" shows, the amount protected from estate tax has varied from year to year and with the winds of political change. The tax rate has also changed from time to time.

B. Gift Tax

Also included in Chart C is the "Gift Tax Exemption" that has been available during these same years. This is the amount of money which, in addition to the "annual exclusion," can be given away without paying any gift or transfer tax. Note that the

17

maximum gift tax exemption amount was $1 million per person from 2002 until 2010, even while the estate tax exemption was dramatically increasing and even eliminated for deaths occurring in 2010. The President and Congress removed the lower $1 million cap on tax-free gifts, replacing it with the $5 million per person gift limit.

The $5 million level of protection was extended in 2012 by last-minute legislation.

CHART C
1990 – 2013: Estate and Gift Tax Protection

Calendar Year	Highest Estate Tax Rate	Estate Tax Exemption	Highest Gift Tax Rate	Gift Tax Exemption
1990-1997	55%	$600,000	55%	$600,000
1998	55%	$625,000	55%	$625,000
1999	55%	$650,000	55%	$650,000
2000	55%	$675,000	55%	$675,000
2001	55%	$675,000	55%	$675,000
2002	50%	$1,000,000	50%	$1,000,000
2003	49%	$1,000,000	49%	$1,000,000
2004	48%	$1,500,000	48%	$1,000,000
2005	47%	$1,500,000	47%	$1,000,000
2006	46%	$2,000,000	46%	$1,000,000
2007	45%	$2,000,000	45%	$1,000,000
2008	45%	$2,000,000	45%	$1,000,000
2009	45%	$3,500,000	45%	$1,000,000
2010	35%	Unlimited	35%	$1,000,000
2011	35%	$5,000,000	35%	$5,000,000

18

| 2012 | 35% | $5,120,000 | 35% | $5,120,000 |
| 2013 | 55% | $5,250,000 | 40% | $5,250,000 |

Reminder: We often use $5,000,000 for simplicity in this book. The actual estate and gift tax protection in 2013 is $5,250,000. It will be adjusted annually and upward under terms of current legislation.

"For the first time in American tax history, an individual can give away at least $5,000,000 without paying gift or any other tax." – M.G.

From a planning perspective, remember that each individual can give away $5 million or pass along $5 million upon death, depending on the year. This means that a couple can pass along over $10 million in 2013 without federal gift or estate tax. With sophisticated planning, as discussed in Chapter 9, dramatically more can be removed from your taxable estate.

C. The Annual Exclusion

No discussion of gifting is complete without attention to the annual exclusion. Best known as the (outdated) $10,000 gifting opportunity, it is now $14,000 in 2013 and will be adjusted upward over time. It lets each of us give away up to $14,000 per year to as many people as we like, without having to report it to the IRS. For further discussion, see Chapter 7, section A.

19

"A gift (beyond $14,000) reduces estate tax protection, dollar for dollar." – M.G.

If a gift is made in excess of the annual exclusion to any one person, it must be reported to the IRS on a Gift Tax Return, Form 709. The IRS effectively keeps track of such gifts because the gift and estate tax protections are "unified." This means that you have a choice: you can either give away $5,250,000 in 2013 and pay no gift tax or you can die in 2013 and your estate pays no estate tax on the first $5,250,000 in your estate. You cannot do both. The combined maximum gift and estate tax exemption is $5,250,000 in 2013. If you give away $5,250,000 this year, you will have zero estate tax protection remaining. Every penny in your estate at the time of death will be exposed to estate tax.

If you use part of your gift exemption during your lifetime, then the unused portion is converted to an estate tax exemption. For example, if you were to make taxable gifts of $1,250,000, then the available estate tax exemption in 2013 would be $4,000,000 ($5,250,000 less $1,250,000).

Could the estate tax protection drop well below $5 million? Yes – See President Obama's 2014 budget.

The White House budget for 2014, released in 2013, seeks to eliminate "a number of loopholes that currently allow wealthy individuals to use sophisticated tax planning to reduce their estate tax liability." The plan seeks to increase tax revenues. Specifically, the President proposes that the level of exemption would drop to $3.5 million in 2018 and that it would not be indexed for inflation. This would represent perhaps a 40% decrease in the level of estate tax protection. The President would also have the estate tax rise to 45% at the highest level.

The White House budget is a wish list. There are many members of Congress who would be eager to make this wish a reality.

The bottom line: We cannot count on the indexed $5 million estate tax protection remaining permanent.

Chapter 4: The Important, but Limited, Role of Revocable Trusts in Estate Tax Planning

Myth: A trust avoids estate tax

Revocable living trusts, also known as *inter vivos* trusts, are excellent planning tools. They ensure the avoidance of probate, which can be unnecessarily costly, time-consuming, and public. They ensure ongoing management of your estate by trusted individuals if you become incapacitated or upon your passing. They do not, however, ensure the avoidance of estate tax.

A. Single Person

For a single person, a revocable trust achieves *no estate tax planning whatsoever*. With or without a trust, an individual can pass along $5,250,000 without estate tax exposure. This level of protection is indexed and will increase annually as estate tax and gift tax law is currently written.

B. Married Couple

The AB Trust, for a married couple, a properly drafted revocable trust can protect the maximum level of protection for each spouse. This is $10,500,000 if death occurs in 2013 or beyond – assuming that there is no change in federal tax legislation. To achieve this protection, alternative approaches can be taken. The most typical approach is to use an AB trust, which mandates the division of the estate into two sub-trusts after the first death. It captures the maximum level of estate tax protection for each spouse, effectively doubling the amount that can pass tax-free.

The AB trust avoids estate tax after the first death because the first decedent takes full advantage of his opportunity to protect $5,250,000. Everything else in the estate avoids estate tax because of the "marital deduction." This means that a married person can leave any amount of money to or for the benefit of the surviving spouse without exposure to any estate tax.

This same result – avoiding all estate tax at the first spouse's death while capturing the basic level of estate tax protection – can be achieved in other ways. Particularly on the East Coast, in non-community property states like New York, estate planning attorneys more typically prepare separate trusts, one for each spouse. The same tax avoidance result is achieved; the same exposure remains.

Example 4-1: Bill Yates and the Marital Deduction

Bill Yates dies and leaves $3 billion to the surviving spouse, Belinda. Because of the "marital deduction," there is no estate tax at the time of his death. The marital deduction provides that any amount of money can be left to a surviving spouse without exposure to estate tax. However, unless proactive planning steps are taken, the IRS will collect estate taxes when Belinda dies.

The following illustration (Illustration I) shows what happens with a $10 million estate if the first death occurs in 2013 and the married couple has an AB Trust. Note that there are no estate taxes whatsoever. Note further that the level of protection for a couple in 2013 is $10,500,000 and will increase annually.

ILLUSTRATION I
AB Trust – Estate Tax Protection in 2013

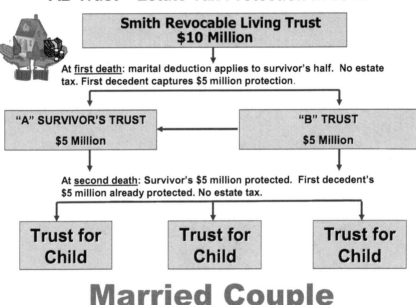

Smith Revocable Living Trust
$10 Million

At <u>first death</u>: marital deduction applies to survivor's half. No estate tax. First decedent captures $5 million protection.

"A" SURVIVOR'S TRUST

$5 Million

"B" TRUST

$5 Million

At <u>second death</u>: Survivor's $5 million protected. First decedent's $5 million already protected. No estate tax.

Trust for Child

Trust for Child

Trust for Child

Married Couple
(2013)

Illustration II is important because it shows what happens if the level of estate tax protection returns to only $1 million. The AB Trust would allow for only $2 million worth of protection from estate tax. It is worth considering because many members of Congress would substantially reduce the level of estate tax protection to increase tax revenues.

ILLUSTRATION II
AB Trust – If Estate Tax Protection is $1 Million

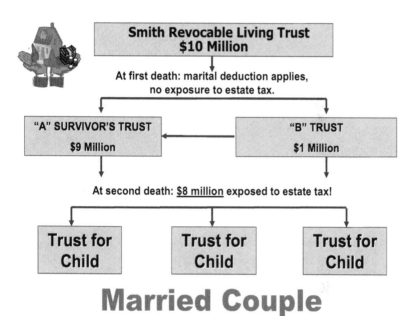

Smith Revocable Living Trust
$10 Million

At first death: marital deduction applies,
no exposure to estate tax.

"A" SURVIVOR'S TRUST

$9 Million

"B" TRUST

$1 Million

At second death: $8 million exposed to estate tax!

Trust for Child

Trust for Child

Trust for Child

Married Couple

Many married individuals want to know that their share of the community property estate will go to their children if they are the first to die. If they do not utilize an AB Trust, all trust assets will be under the control of the survivor, who can amend the trust and modify the distribution plan. Put more simply, the survivor could change the distribution plan to exclude all or some of the children, perhaps in favor of a new spouse, new stepchildren, or favored charitable entities.

With the AB Trust, the B Trust – holding the first decedent's half of the estate – is irrevocable. This means that, if the trust provides for distribution to the children at the time of the second death, all assets in the B Trust will go to the children. The survivor can change the distribution plan with regard to her half of the estate, which is in the A Trust, but nothing more.

1. Rational for Simplifying Your Trust – Eliminating the AB Trust Approach

If you are a couple and your estate is under $5 million, should you do an AB Trust? If you are a couple and your estate is well under $5 million, consider simplifying your trust so that it does not divide into two sub-trusts (A and B) after the first death. Rather, your trust can provide that the trust remains intact "as is" with the surviving spouse controlling trust assets and having unlimited access to them. This avoids the need to divide the estate into two sub-trusts, a process that involves consideration of multiple issues. It also gives the surviving spouse unlimited control of remaining assets, arguably a significant benefit.

2. Benefit of AB Trust – Your Estate May Grow

Your estate may not be exposed to estate tax under current legislation. This does not mean, however, that you should ignore tax planning opportunities and opt for a simplistic approach. Your estate could grow to the point where there is estate tax exposure. Legislative changes could dramatically reduce the level of protection. Beyond that, you must think about minimizing or eliminating estate tax exposure for your children and grandchildren. This can be done by the use of Family Protection or Dynasty Trusts. This is discussed in Chapter 8.

You should also consider planning steps that enable you to transfer assets from your estate to the next generation in a safe, protective manner so that future growth will not create tax liability.

For example, you may have stock in a new company that is valued at $200,000. If the company does well, those assets could later be worth $10 million. If you transfer all or a portion of those assets to dynasty trusts for the next generation, two powerful protections are captured. First, growth in the value of the estate occurred in the hands of the next generation, not in yours. If you retain those assets, perhaps 40% of the value would be lost to estate tax.

Secondly, by utilizing dynasty trust planning, the full value is protected for the grandchildren because of generation skipping transfer tax protection that is captured in this planning approach. Literally millions of dollars are saved for following generations.

C. Your Revocable Living Trust Is *Not* "One Size Fits All"

No family is "plain vanilla." Every family has its issues. Estate and tax planning must be sensitive to these issues.

You understand that a revocable trust is typically the cornerstone of your estate plan. This does not mean that your trust can be drafted online or by software that only takes into account the size of your estate and fundamental facts about your family.

While such approaches are highly efficient and no doubt cost-effective, they do you a tremendous disservice.

I believe that this field of law should be known as "family law," a term unfortunately captured, in a stroke of marketing genius, by attorneys who handle divorces. It is our field of law that so strongly reinforces family values and responds to the reality of family dynamics.

To properly prepare a revocable trust – and other elements of an estate plan – there must be an open discussion about family members.
Achievements must be understood by the drafting attorney. Special worries must be identified and addressed. Same-sex couples and non-citizens face other planning issues.

> ### No family is "plain vanilla."
> ### Every family has its issues.

1. <u>Same-Sex Couples</u>. Federal law now provides that a legally married, same-sex couple enjoys the same gift and estate tax protections as a heterosexual couple. This means that a same-sex couple can enjoy the tax planning advantages of an AB Trust and the "marital deduction." The marital deduction provides that any amount of money can be left to a surviving spouse without exposure to estate tax.

In simple summary, the same planning opportunities available to heterosexual couples are now available to same-sex married couples, provided that they are legally married. Previously, because the marital deduction – and the AB Trust – was not available to same-sex couples, each spouse would prepare his or her own estate plan, typically retaining assets as separate property. New planning opportunities therefore exist and will provide for dramatically expanded gift and estate tax protections.

2. <u>Non-US citizen surviving spouse</u>. Noncitizens may not take advantage of the marital deduction. However, in 2013, there is an annual gifting exclusion of $143,000 for gifts made to a non-U.S. citizen spouse. Furthermore, a noncitizen may take full advantage of the $5,250,000 gifting opportunity in 2013. Both of these figures are adjusted annually and will increase in the future under current law. To address estate tax exposure, when the surviving spouse is not a citizen, a Qualified Domestic Trust (QDOT) is typically appropriate.

3. <u>The spendthrift child</u>. Your son is a well-educated, wonderful person. He would give you the shirt off his back. In fact, he has often given the shirt off his back to needy friends and acquaintances. His good heart makes him a logical target for those who would take advantage of him. You can protect his inherited assets from his wonderful naiveté by restricting his access to inherited assets. This would likely be a trust managed by some other individual or entity. In effect, he would be given an allowance but have very limited to access underlying assets. Terms of such a trust are individualized, depending on the actual history and circumstances.

4. <u>The Special Needs Child</u>. If a child is disabled, meaning that he is unable to obtain and maintain employment, he may qualify for a number of government programs. Supplemental Security Income (SSI) will give him a monthly income even if he has no work history. Medicaid, known as Medi-Cal in California, will provide him with a comprehensive, if imperfect health insurance program to ensure his medical care. Housing subsidies may enable him to obtain safe, accessible housing. He may need to live in a long-term care or otherwise supported environment. These programs are typically available only to those who have limited means.

A Special Needs Trust is appropriate for this individual. It can hold any amount of money without disturbing eligibility for government programs. See Gilfix, Michael *Special Needs Trust Creation and Management Guide,* 2013, Gilfix & La Poll.[1]

> *You will roll over in your grave if your son-in-law – you never liked him anyway – drives away from the divorce court in a new Tesla that he bought with your money.*

5. <u>The child in the imperfect marriage</u>. You are worried that your daughter will inherit assets from you, share them with her husband, and later endure a divorce. You will roll over in your grave if your son-in-law – you never liked him anyway – drives away from the divorce court in a new Tesla that he bought with

---

[1] To obtain this practical publication about managing Special Needs Trusts, contact Gilfix & La Poll at 650-493-8070 or www.Gilfix.com.

your money. A properly drafted Family Protection or Dynasty Trust established for the benefit of your daughter will protect inherited assets from this outcome. In effect, you are preparing a prenuptial or postnuptial agreement for your daughter with regard to inherited assets. See Chapter 8, which discusses Family Protection or Dynasty Trusts in greater detail.

6. The child exposed to litigation. Your son may work in a field with a high incidence of litigation. He may be a soils engineer or a plastic surgeon. If you leave assets directly to him, those assets are exposed if he is ever sued. By utilizing a Family Protection or Dynasty Trust, those assets enjoy a very high level of protection from litigation. Alternatively or additionally, you may want to establish a Domestic Asset Protection Trust (DAPT) in a state that allows such trusts. These trusts enable you to transfer your own assets into a trust that will provide substantial protection from litigation against you. The benefits are then enjoyed by the next generation.

7. The wonderful, but slightly irresponsible child. Assets must be nurtured, protected, and invested if they are to last a lifetime and be preserved for following generations. If a child is simply unable to do this, another individual or entity may be named as trustee of a trust established for his benefit. The child may be given some level of control, but financially significant actions might require two signatures or the exclusive responsibility of the professional trustee.

8. Pet Trusts. Let's face it. Many of us have closer relationships with our pets than we do with our own children. Many of us do not have children. It is possible to establish a trust to ensure that our pets will be well cared for if they survive us.

31

9. The outcast child. A child may be estranged from you or the entire family. You may exclude this child as a beneficiary. You may condition inheritance on certain changes and behavior. This is a complicated area of law, one that must be addressed with great care and sophistication.

10. The troubled child. A child may have substance abuse problems, move from religious cult to religious cult, or otherwise lead a troubled, challenging existence. A trust can provide for distributions to such a child only if certain benchmarks are obtained and achieved.

In conclusion, a revocable trust is not a "one size fits all" document.

Use online trust services at your peril.

Sophisticated consumers know better, but it can be tempting to avoid the cost of a skilled and experienced estate planning attorney. Online services do not pretend to offer tax planning advice. They stick with the "basics," which may be adequate for individuals with small estates. Even then, scores of difficult questions are not asked, as this would make simple "fill out the form" planning impossible.

For example, individuals utilizing this approach are asked to identify successor trustees. The challenging and demanding responsibilities of serving as a successor trustee are not explained. The "pros and cons" of naming two children, for example, as a co-trustees are not explained. Experienced estate planning attorneys often devote 15 to 30 minute discussions to this topic alone because it is so important.

Countless other issues require discussion and thoughtful resolution. More time may be devoted to choosing your next automobile than to terms of your revocable trust, which is profoundly important for the benefit of your spouse, your children, and your grandchildren.

You have worked a lifetime to grow your estate. You want to protect it for your family for generations. You can only do this if you get good advice from a truly qualified attorney. See Chapter 4 or 10 to get even more perspective.

Chapter 5: Portability – If a Needed AB Trust Was Not In Place

Fortunately, Congress provided in 2010 that estate tax protections available to an individual can be preserved even if the individual did not take traditional, appropriate planning steps. Assume that a couple has a $9 million estate and did no trust planning whatsoever. After the first death, the entire estate belongs to the survivor. Upon her death, only $5,250,000 will be protected from estate tax exposure. Approximately $4 million will be exposed to estate tax. The resulting tax would be approximately $1.6 million.

Portability allows the surviving spouse to take advantage of the estate tax protection opportunity that the decedent had available to her. This means that over $10 million can still be protected from estate tax exposure.

It is vitally important to understand that portability is not automatically available. The surviving spouse must take appropriate, formal, and sophisticated steps to be certain that this opportunity is preserved.

Most fundamentally, the surviving spouse must file an estate tax return (Form 709) after the first death even though no tax is owed. This must be filed within nine months of the first death. If this step is not taken, portability – and perhaps millions of dollars of estate tax protection – is lost.

> *It is vitally important to understand that portability is not automatically available.*

Chapter 6: You Can Plan to Avoid the Estate Tax. Overcoming Inertia; Overcoming Objections.

"You can protect the family home. You can protect the family business. You can probably protect everything." – M.G.

A. Addressing Objections

Most people do nothing to avoid the estate tax. This delights the IRS and the U.S. Treasury, which receives your **estate** tax money. It does not delight your children. It would make you roll over in your grave if you could see it happen. If you think about it, not planning is a way of planning to make substantial gifts to the IRS.

Here are the most typical reasons, beyond the powers of inertia and ignorance, why people fail to plan.

1. You may say "I'll be gone. What do I care?"

2. You may be unwilling to pay legal fees.

3. You may be unwilling to give up control of your assets.

4. You may feel that you need to keep your money for travel, enjoyment, and the cost of long-term care.

Let's address these very logical thoughts.

> **If you think about it, not planning is a way of planning to make substantial gifts to the IRS.**

1. What do I care? Let the kids deal with it

"Death is the most convenient time to tax rich people."
— David Lloyd George

It is your privilege to do as little or as much planning as you wish. You must, however, consider the consequences of inaction. The following examples may surprise you. I admit it: They are designed to shake you out of complacency.

Example 6-1: the $1 million house

Mrs. Jones has lived simply all her life. Thirty years ago, she bought a nice house in a wonderful neighborhood. She reluctantly acknowledges that it is worth $1 million in today's market. She also built up a $400,000 IRA. She has another $200,000 in savings and investments. She lives frugally and does not see herself as a "rich person." She had a local attorney prepare a simple will. Mrs. Jones dies in 2013. She would be shocked to know that her estate will go through probate with legal fees in excess of $30,000. With a revocable trust, these fees would be dramatically reduced.

<u>Example 6-2: the $1 million life insurance policy</u>

Mr. and Mrs. Smith believe that they have a $6 million estate. They own their valuable home and a nice cabin in the mountains. They have two savings accounts and a stock portfolio valued at $1.5 million. These assets are valued at over $6 million. They created an AB trust and believe that there will be no estate tax.

They have a $1 million life insurance policy naming their children as beneficiaries. They never thought of this as an asset because "it goes to the children." They were also told that the life insurance policy is "tax-free" when they purchased it and made their premium payments. The information they were given about tax was only half right. Receipt of a life insurance death benefit is free from income tax exposure. Unfortunately, however, the $1 million death benefit is counted as part of their taxable estate.

Because their estate is therefore valued at over $6 million, the *estate tax will be approximately $400,000 at* the time of the second death. Use of an Irrevocable Life Insurance Trust (ILIT) would have avoided all estate tax.

"You may not care, but your kids will. They may even be willing to pay for good advice! After all, the planning is for them." – M.G.

<u>Example 6-3: the $13 million estate</u>

Mr. and Mrs. K have a $13 million estate and understand that the tax exposure is approximately $1 million. They profess disinterest–"it's the kids' problem."

Objectively, it is wise to be conservative and plan for the worst while hoping for the best. This means that planning steps should be taken. If you view it as "the kids' problem," involve them in the process and let them know about the tax exposure. If they are financially able, they may be willing to pay for tax advice on your behalf.

"But why should the frugal and thrifty among the rich be taxed heavily on their death beds, while the spendthrifts who live luxuriously are not?" – Edward J. McCaffery

2. Think about the grandkids

"Your kids are OK–they have their issues. But the grandkids are perfect!" – M.G.

Unless your children are very secure financially, inheritance matters. You may feel that they will get along just fine, regardless of what you leave them. But if you think about the possible needs of your grandchildren and great-grandchildren, you may come to a different conclusion.

The cost of living and the cost of housing, in particular, are prohibitively high in many communities. Yet, we want our children and grandchildren to live nearby. We may have to help them with a down payment on a home they otherwise could not afford. This is critically important for our quality of life.

"Study after study shows that we are healthier and happier if our kids live nearby and are part of our everyday lives." – M.G.

If you do not want to deal with estate tax for the benefit of your children, do so for the benefit of your grandchildren. You may help pay for the best quality education, regardless of expense. This also means that you will also include Dynasty Trusts in your estate plan for the benefit of your children–to avoid estate tax exposure when they pass, in the distant future. See Chapter 8.

"Don't have children. Have grandchildren."
– Gore Vidal

3. You are reluctant or unwilling to pay legal fees

"That's how smart people avoid tax and keep their money. They throw a few bucks at attorneys and CPAs and get good advice." – Len Tillem, lawyer and radio talk show host

It does cost money to plan properly. It can be challenging to write that check to pay the lawyer, particularly since you live frugally "and have kept every Cool Whip container that crossed your threshold!"[1]

The problem is that you must actually write a check to pay for legal advice, while the dramatically

---

[1] This imaginative statement was made by radio talk show host Len Tillem in 2011.

higher costs of other professional services are effectively invisible even though you are, in fact, paying them.

Let's get some perspective on this question of attorney fees. Consider the very real case of Mr. and Mrs. H.

Example 6-4: Getting perspective on professional fees

Mr. H has a $6 million estate. He has $2 million under professional management. Also, he just sold his $2 million house and is now living in a continuing care retirement community (CCRC).

He is worried about estate tax exposure. He understands that exposure approaches $1 million. He saw a skilled, competent tax attorney, who said the fees for a plan to address tax planning would likely exceed $10,000.[1]

Mr. H was outraged. He shopped around and found an attorney who said it would cost only $4,000 to do his trust and estate planning. He hired this attorney, paid $4,000, and was very gratified.

So Mr. H saved $6,000 on legal fees and achieved no tax planning. He accepted over $1 million in estate tax exposure. *A $10,000 investment in sophisticated planning would have saved as much as $2 million in estate*

---

[1] Tax advice of this nature is typically tax deductible, so the net fee is dramatically less.

tax. But Mr. H refused to pay it.

Did Mr. H think about other fees that he is paying?

His **money manager** charges a fee of 1% of managed assets each year. He is paying his money manager $20,000 per year. On top of that, the mutual funds in which his assets were placed generated additional management fees. The money manager has not been great, underperforming the S&P 500 by 2%. "An Index fund would have better," Mr. H says. Over the last 5 years, his money manager's fees exceeded $100,000. But Mr. H never had to write a check since the fees were periodically deducted from his account. The same is true for mutual fund fees that never see the light of day. He did not think about these fees and did not complain.

So, some $270,000 in money management and realtor fees and annuity commissions were paid by Mr. H without a thought. Yet, he refused to pay $10,000 for tax planning and advice that would save his family as much as $2 million.

Realtor fees for the sale of his house were 6% of the $2 million purchase price. The house sold within one week of going on the market. "It sold itself," says Mr. H, because of its location and condition. Realtor fees were $120,000. It never occurred to Mr. H to negotiate these fees. He did not have to write a check, as the realtors collected fees out of escrow. He did not complain about this $120,000 fee.

With some proceeds of the house sale, Mr. H decided to invest in an annuity. He contacted his **insurance agent**, who sold him the annuity. The commission collected by the insurance agent was $30,000. Mr. H did not have to write a check, so he did not complain. The fee was invisible.

So, some $270,000 in money management and realtor fees and annuity commissions were paid by Mr. H without a thought. Yet, he refused to pay $10,000 for tax planning and advice that would save his family as much as $2 million.

"We pay more attention to the cost of toilet paper than we do to the cost and benefits of tax advice." – M.G.

4. <u>You are unwilling to give up control of your assets</u>

You may be comfortable with the idea of giving up ownership or control of significant assets if there is a significant tax advantage in doing so.

Alternatively, it may make you uncomfortable. This is perhaps more likely if you have business or rental properties that you own and actively manage. More simply, you may not like the idea of giving up ownership because it would make you feel less independent, less in control. Perhaps you would feel too dependent on your children if you give a substantial portion of your estate to them.

"'A gift is a gift. There can be no strings attached.' Not necessarily so!" – Francis A. La Poll, Esq.

If you make simple, direct gifts to your children, you have given up ownership and control. But there are other ways of removing assets from your estate without giving up control. For example, you can place rental properties in a family limited partnership, give your children up to 99% of the partnership, but *keep control and a substantial management fee by being the general partner.* You can achieve this same result with other planning tools, as well.

5. <u>You want to keep your money for travel, enjoyment, and the cost of long-term care</u>

You want to do tax planning, and you trust your kids, but you have a lot of life left to live. You want to have ample resources under your control so that you can pay for any enjoyable activity, including international travel, that strikes your fancy. You want to do as you please!

You may also be concerned about the cost of long-term care, which can include help at home, assisted living, residential care, and skilled nursing care.

It is indeed fundamental that you should have freedom from financial worries as you live your life. Tax planning is not an "all or nothing" proposition. Rather, it is a matter of identifying your goals and crafting a plan that accommodates as many of them as possible.

Here are some approaches you could take:

• Retain significant assets, notwithstanding tax implications.

- Convey assets to your children, who then place some or most of them in a trust or trusts established for your benefit. There will therefore be ample resources available for anything you need, with a focus on maintaining your current standard of living.

- Develop a comprehensive plan, using the planning tools in Chapters 5, 9, and 10 to achieve the plan that most pleases you.

- Many other approaches can be taken.

B. Planning for Long-Term Care

Anything can happen. Even we Boomers have to acknowledge this truth. High-quality long-term care services may prove to be essential. You may need help at home from a professional caregiver. You may need to live in an assisted living facility, where help is available if you need it. At some point, you may need to be in a skilled nursing facility. All of these are expensive, costing as much as $10,000 per month or more. In New York City, for example, some skilled nursing facilities cost over $15,000 per month.

Consider purchasing long-term care insurance. Comprehensive policies allow you to use the benefits for home care, assisted living, or skilled nursing care.

If you do not have such insurance when you need it, you will either have to pay out of your own pocket (self-insure) or qualify for Medicaid, known as Medi-Cal in California. It can pay all or most of the cost of nursing home care. Medicaid typically does not pay for assisted living. In most states, it does not pay for home care services, except on a very limited basis. New York is one exception.

Asset Protection, Medi-Cal Planning

Here is the message: if you face or your parent faces long-term care, you can protect your assets and qualify for Medicaid, known as Medi-Cal in California. Contact the office of Gilfix & La Poll if this issue arises. Many planning options exist. It is particularly important to protect your residence.

Chapter 7: Estate Tax Planning – The Fundamentals of Transferred Wealth

For assets to be exposed to the estate tax, they must be in your "estate" at the time of your death. If they are removed from your estate prior to your death, they avoid this tax.

If it were this easy, you would simply give away all of your assets before your passing and eliminate this tax. It is not this simple; there are limitations on gifting. Yet, it can be done.

If you give away too much money to take advantage of appropriate tools, or do it incorrectly, you may have to pay a "gift tax."[1] This tax is the same as the estate tax rate, 40% in the year 2013 and going forward.

Here are some of the more obvious, fundamental steps that can be taken to reduce the size of your taxable estate.

A. The Annual Exclusion

You can give away up to $14,000 per year – to each of as many people as you like – without having to report it to the IRS. This is the "annual exclusion" amount in 2013. It will increase in future years. Such gifts have no impact on your lifetime gift and estate

---

[1] A **federal gift tax return** (Form 709) must be filed with the IRS if you gift more than $14,000 to any individual in a calendar year. This tax return reports such gifts and indicates why no gift tax has to be paid. This annual exclusion figure may be larger in the future.

tax protection. A married couple can therefore give $28,000 to each of their children and each of their grandchildren year after year without reporting such gifts. In fact, these gifts can be made to anyone, regardless of his or her relationship to you.

Receipt of these gifts, like the receipt of all gifts, is not a taxable event. The recipient simply keeps and enjoys the money.

If you make gifts – make no mistakes!

Cost Basis

If you transfer assets other than cash, note that the recipient takes your "cost basis" in the gifted assets. While rarely a reason to forego gifting when estate taxes are to be avoided, it is a factor to consider.

Special Needs Trust

If you have a child or grandchild with special needs, gifts should not be made directly to that child. Instead, a Special Needs Trust should be created for the benefit of the child, and assets are transferred to that trust.

Dynasty Trust

Most gifts or transfers should be made to Dynasty Trusts. See Chapter 8.

The simplest way to use this opportunity is to give cash. You can be more creative and give away stock, partnership interests, and fractional interests in real property.

Be careful about using *Uniform Transfer to Minors Act (UTMA)* accounts for these gifts, though bank tellers so often recommend them. If you do, you will likely be advised to serve as "custodian" of such accounts. This sounds good because you will have the power to decide if and how to invest the money. There are, however, two potential problems.

First, the full value of these accounts are counted as part of your taxable estate if you die while still serving as custodian. If you have a taxable estate, $100,000 in such accounts will generate estate tax in the area of $40,000. This is tax on money you do not even own!

Second, your kids or grandkids receive the money when they are either 18 or 21. Is that wise? Will the money go to scuba gear, a hot car (the "Lamborghini Effect"), or be used for drugs or alcohol? Will the recipient drop out of college "just for a while" to backpack in Europe?

It is typically better to give to trusts or other entities that will allow you or some other trusted person to control the funds. The trust can end when the child attains a more mature age and the trust assets are then distributed to him. Alternatively, the trust can allow the trustee to decide how to use the money and when the young beneficiary is to be given control by becoming trustee of his own trust.

"Annual exclusion" gifts cannot be made to either Special Needs Trusts or Dynasty Trusts. They can be made to properly drafted "Crummey Trusts," a topic beyond the scope of this book.

B. The Remarkable $5 million Giving Opportunity. Should You Do It Now?

In 2013, you can give away up to $5,250,000 without paying any gift tax. As with annual exclusion gifts, receipt of such gifts is not a taxable event. There is no income tax to pay. This means that a married couple can give away over $10 million in 2013. With sophisticated planning, described below, substantially more can in fact be given and, thereby, removed from your taxable estate.

Such gifts must be reported on a gift tax return (I.R.S. Form 709). If you use this giving opportunity, you are exhausting your estate tax protection on a dollar for dollar basis.

Note that the $5 million gift and estate tax protection, adjusted upward annually, is now "permanent" tax law. Major gifting is therefore, not a necessary step to avoid tax. This amount can be passed along upon death without estate tax. Some, however, worry that the law can change and want to take advantage of this remarkable opportunity now.

Example 7-1: $4 million estate, $4 million gift

Ms. Johnson has a $4 million estate and gives away her entire estate in 2013 to her two children. She reports the gifts to the IRS. No tax is paid. While her estate is not likely to face estate tax exposure if she did not make these gifts, all assets are now in the estates of her children – or, better, in their dynasty trusts. The value can grow without limit and face no estate tax upon Ms. Johnson's passing even if the assets have grown to over $6 million.

Example 7-2: $6 million estate, $5 million gift

Mr. Long had a $6 million estate and gave $5 million to his children in 2012. He reported the gift to the IRS. His remaining estate is subject to estate tax, but the $5 million previously transferred – plus growth in the value of those assets – escapes estate tax exposure. He can protect the balance of his estate from tax by using any or all three approaches:

> *Option One*: Annual exclusion gifts to children, grandchildren, and others.

> *Option Two*: Make additional gifts as the tax protected amount increases annually. In 2013, $5,250,000 is the lifetime level of protection, so one can give away another $250,000 without gift tax exposure.

> *Option Three*: Take advantage of tax planning techniques identified in this chapter.

The tax avoidance benefits of this opportunity are enormous. They should be considered by every unmarried person with an estate in excess of $3 million. They should be considered by every couple with an estate in excess of perhaps $6 million.

Such giving must also be carefully considered. It should not be done if you will lose sleep at night or otherwise compromise your quality of life.

C. Pay Tuition for Relatives, Anyone

You may pay the cost of tuition for anyone, related or not. This includes preschool and elementary school, as well as college and postgraduate education. You must pay the institution directly, rather than give your grandchild the money and have him or her pay the tuition. This is separate from and in addition to all other planning options.

This opportunity does not include the cost of room and board.

D. Pay Medical Bills for Relatives, Anyone

You may pay medical bills for anyone. You must directly pay the provider–the physician, the hospital, and/or the clinic. There is no limit and doing so does not erode or reduce your lifetime gift and estate tax protections.

Remember: do not give the money to the individual who incurred the bill so she can pay it. Leave her out of it and pay the bill directly.

Chapter 8: Dynasty or Family Protection Trusts – Dynamic Generational Planning

Dynasty Trusts "offer big tax savings and can help protect family money from creditors and ex-spouses."
– Wall Street Journal, August 20, 2003

This is a trust that you must establish for the benefit of your child or children. The only exception, parenthetically, is if you have a child with special needs, in which case a Special Needs Trust is required.

When you leave assets to your children, there are two alternative approaches that you can take. You can leave the assets directly to them or you can leave assets to a trust or trusts you establish for their benefit. If you leave the assets directly to them, they have complete control of those assets. They are exposed to litigation and other potential assaults. More importantly, the assets become part of your children's estates. Upon their passing, all of these assets are again exposed to estate tax.

"Whenever possible, we take a multi-generational approach." – M.G.

The alternative is to establish a Family Protection Trust™, also known as a Dynasty Trust, for the benefit of each child. We recommend this approach because of the benefits and protections derived from such trusts. These protections are in three powerful areas.

A. Divorce Protection: "Pre-Nup" or "Post-Nup" Planning for Your Kids and Grandkids

Any divorce attorney will tell you that, after a married person inherits assets, all or most of those assets will be held in both names after a few years go by. This happens because life goes on, not because the son-in-law or daughter-in-law is a conniving person. Your child and her husband may move their assets to a new entity, such as Schwab, or put them under management with a new money manager. When this is done, they will be asked how the accounts are to be titled. A couple's assets are somewhat logically presumed to be shared assets in such circumstances. It may automatically be placed in both names.

They may also decide to buy a new house or a second property. A title company may automatically put such property in both names, sometimes asking and sometimes not. The point is that inherited assets, more typically than not, end up in both your child's name and his or her spouse's name. If there is ever a divorce, those assets are divided equally. Half of your child's inherited assets can be lost in divorce proceedings.

"You would roll over in your grave!" – M.G.

If you instead leave assets to Dynasty Trusts established for the benefit of your son or daughter, the assets are segregated and will remain with your child even if he or she someday endures a divorce. The assets are therefore preserved for your child and your grandchildren. They remain in your "bloodline."

> **The assets are segregated and will remain with your child even if he or she someday endures a divorce.**

In a very real sense, creating such trusts is tantamount to preparing an antenuptial (also known as a prenuptial) or postnuptial agreement for your child. You will spare your child the need to have a difficult discussion with his or her spouse about why assets cannot be placed into both of their names. When asked, your daughter replies: "I would love to, but I can't. Everything is in an irrevocable trust and I can't change its terms." Let her (gratefully) blame you!

B. Litigation Protection

If you leave assets directly to your child, they will be in his name and exposed to collection if someone successfully sues him. If you instead leave assets in a Dynasty Trust, they enjoy a very high level of asset protection. This is because the assets do not belong to your child. A person successfully suing your daughter will then have to commence a separate action in an effort to break the trust and reach trust assets. At minimum, this structure provides enormous settlement value, as do offshore trusts.

Litigation protection is maximized if someone other than your child serves as trustee of the Dynasty Trust. In most situations, however, litigation is not a major fear and it is appropriate to let your child serve as trustee, perhaps stepping aside as trustee during the pendency of any legal proceedings if there is a challenge.

The extent of litigation protection depends on the law in your state and how the trust is written.

C. Estate Tax Protection for Your Children and Grandchildren

This is the best known benefit of a Dynasty Trust. It also explains why such trusts are sometimes referred to as "GST" trusts or "generation-skipping" trusts.

> Example 8-1: Saving millions for the grandkids – GST tax planning
>
> You transfer $5 million to a properly drafted Dynasty Trust for the benefit of your son in the year 2012. Only somewhat optimistically, assume that the $5 million asset grows to be worth $12 million at the time of your son's passing in the distant future. *The full $12 million will pass intact for the benefit of your son's children, your grandchildren. None of it will be exposed to estate tax.* This quite literally achieves the avoidance of almost $5 million in estate tax.

Tax law includes a "generation-skipping transfer" tax. If you transfer too much to your grandchildren, this 35% GST tax is imposed on top of and in addition to the gift tax. Generally speaking, the amount that can be passed along to or for the benefit of grandchildren without exposure to this tax is the same as the level of estate tax protection. Since $5,250,000 is protected from GST tax exposure in

2013, that amount can be conveyed to a Dynasty Trust. These assets, including their growth, will not be included in the estates of your child or your grandchildren, since the Dynasty Trust structure remains in place for them, as well.

Example 8-2: Allocating GST Tax (2013); $3 Million Estate

You transfer $3 million to a Dynasty Trust for the benefit of your daughter. The full $3 million will enjoy GST protection. The entire amount, perhaps $7 million or $8 million at the time of your daughter's death, will pass without exposure to estate tax. See the following illustration.

ILLUSTRATION III
2013 DYNASTY TRUST GST ALLOCATION
Gift to Trust: $3 Million

GST Tax Protected $3 million	Unprotected by GST Protection: $0
-- Unlimited Growth (e.g. $7-8 million)	-- Zero because under $5 million transferred
-- Excluded from daughter's taxable estate	
-- Passes to her children free of tax	

57

Get it? ***This can be millions and millions of dollars protected from estate tax exposure for your future great grandchildren and beyond. What a legacy!***

Tax laws can change. It is entirely possible that the level of estate tax protection will be lower in future years.

If the level of estate tax protection is only $3.5 million, as it could someday be, only $3.5 million could then be passed along to a Dynasty Trust to capture this benefit. If an estate is valued at $4 million at the time of death, only the $3.5 million would capture this tax protection even though the entire amount would go into the Dynasty Trust. The entire amount would enjoy divorce and litigation protection benefits, but $500,000 (in this example) would be included in the child's taxable estate at the time of his or her passing.

*   *   *

1. <u>Who will be the trustee of this trust</u>? If your child is a capable money manager, he or she can be the trustee of her own trust. If there is some question about ability to manage assets, you can name another individual or entity to serve as trustee or co-trustee.

2. <u>Rule Against Perpetuities</u>: In most states, these trusts and the estate tax protection lasts for perhaps three generations. It is limited by the "Rule Against Perpetuities." Some states have eliminated or substantially extended the Rule, allowing Dynasty Trusts and their tax and other protections to last for multiple generations.

Regardless of whether you fund Dynasty Trusts by gift or bequest, they are an essential component of a good estate plan. Throughout this publication, we assume that they will be integrated into your planning.

President Obama's 2014 Budget Calls for Limiting GST/Dynasty Trust Tax Protection

The President is well aware of the fact that some states have passed legislation allowing dynasty trusts to last hundreds of years. One state allows such trusts to last forever, forever protecting trust assets from estate tax exposure, regardless of how large they grow. The President's budget statement proposes that the duration of dynasty trusts should be limited to 90 years. This is even shorter than the current, relatively typical law which provides that such trusts are ruled by the "rule against perpetuity," which can allow such trusts to last for 100-110 years in many circumstances.

Advanced Estate Planning
What You Can Do to Protect Your Estate

"...to arrange his affairs that his taxes shall be as low as possible; he is not bound to choose that pattern which will best pay the Treasury; there is not even a patriotic duty to increase one's taxes." –
Learned Hand, renowned federal judge

This chapter introduces you to the more powerful planning approaches that can reduce or eliminate estate tax. They complement the "basic" planning steps outlined in Chapter 7. Charitable giving is discussed in Section G, below. Sophisticated charitable giving can provide tax and other rewarding benefits.

If you have an estate that is of such size that a portion could be exposed to the punishing 40% estate tax this chapter is required reading.

A. The Irrevocable Life Insurance Trust – Supercharging Inherited Wealth

You may have been advised to purchase a $2 million life insurance policy so that your children will have liquid assets to pay the estate tax that will be due upon your death. If you do this, you are compounding the estate tax problem, not addressing it.

Life insurance death benefits are part of your taxable estate if you had any "incidents of ownership" in the policy: The $2 million in death benefits is added to other assets that you own as the total value of your estate is calculated. The $2 million life insurance policy will itself generate some $800,000 in estate tax exposure if you have a taxable estate.

You have such "incidents of ownership" if you own the policy, pay the premiums, or reserve the right to change the beneficiaries. Even if you do not, the entire amount can become part of your estate if you name your "estate" as the beneficiary of your policy.

If, however, you create an irrevocable life insurance trust (ILIT) and properly manage it, the death benefit will not be included as part of your estate, regardless of how large it is. If you have a $2 million life insurance policy, the full $2 million is distributed to the beneficiaries. If you have a $10 million life insurance policy, the full $10 million is distributed to the beneficiaries intact.

This irrevocable trust is typically established by you. You name an independent third party to be the trustee of the trust.

The trustee obtains a life insurance policy on your life. Each year, you write checks to the trustee in amounts that typically do not exceed $14,000 ($28,000 if married) for every individual who is named as a beneficiary of the trust.

You explain to the trustee in writing that these gifts are available to the individuals, presumably your children or grandchildren. The trustee informs your children or grandchildren of these gifts and gives them the opportunity to withdraw the money. If they do not, the trustee can use those funds to pay the annual premiums. These are often referred t as "Crummey Trust" provisions.

By actually making these funds available to the beneficiaries, they qualify for the $14,000 "annual exclusion." The transferred funds are, therefore, removed from your estate and efficiently utilized to pay life insurance premiums. Because you have no "incidents of ownership" over the policy that is owned by the insurance trust, the death benefit is not part of your taxable estate.

Example 9-1: $5 million ILIT

Mr. Wong creates an ILIT, naming his daughter as the trustee. The trustee obtains a $5 million life insurance policy on Mr. Wong, who must pass a physical examination and otherwise qualify for life insurance. The annual premiums are $56,000. Mr. Wong has four children. He writes four checks in the amount of $14,000 made payable to his trust. He instructs the trustee in writing that these gifts are for his children. The trustee writes a letter to each child, informing the child of the gift and of the opportunity to request and obtain the money from the trustee. The children are given 30 days to claim their money. They do not. (They know that if they were to claim the $14,000, there would be no further annual contributions and they might even be disinherited.) The trustee then uses the $56,000 to pay the annual premium. This is done year after year, with careful and appropriate documentation.

<u>Result</u>: Even though Mr. Wong has a large, taxable estate at the time of his death, the $5 million death benefit is distributed to his children, $1 million each, completely free from estate tax exposure.

<u>Example 9-2: $30 million Super-Charged ILIT</u>

This example supercharges insurance and ILIT planning.

Assume that Mr. Black's estate is valued at $30 million. He knows that the estate tax approaches $10 million if his death occurs in 2013, when only $5,250,000 can be protected. He decides to transfer $5 million worth of assets to an Irrevocable Life Insurance Trust, virtually exhausting most of his lifetime gifting opportunity. Using income from ILIT assets, the trustee of the trust obtains and pays annual premiums on a $10 million life insurance policy. Remaining in his estate is $25 million.

Interest earned by the $5 million – $250,000 per year if it earns 5% – is sufficient to pay the annual premiums.

If Mr. Black does nothing further, $25 million is exposed to estate tax if death occurs in 2013 or thereafter. The tax is approximately $10 million. Not included in his estate, and therefore protected for the next generation, are both the $10 million life insurance benefit and the $5 million originally transferred into the ILIT. By this approach, he increases the assets left for the benefit of his children by approximately 50%.

ILLUSTRATION IV
Single client Mr. Black
Estimated Net Worth: $30,000,000
How much will be left in the Estate?

	2012: Tax Planning with ILIT	2013: No Tax Planning
Estimated Net Worth	**$30,000,000**	**$30,000,000**
Exemption	- $5,000,000	- $5,000,000
Taxable Estate	$25,000,000	$25,000,000
40% Estate Tax (2013)	$10,000,000	$10,000,000
Subtotal	$15,000,000	$15,000,000
Add back	$5,000,000	$5,000,000
Add in tax-free life insurance	$10,000,000	
TOTAL LEFT IN ESTATE	**$30,000,000**	**$20,000,000**

NET: $10,000,000 more is preserved with ILIT Planning

Use of Dynasty or Family Protection Trust: As described in Chapter 8, you will create one Dynasty Trust for the benefit of each of your children, so ILIT proceeds go not to your children but to their Dynasty Trusts. The insurance trust will name the Dynasty Trust as beneficiaries. In this way, inherited assets can avoid exposure to estate tax when the children pass. This can save them and the grandchildren millions of dollars in estate tax.

Indeed, virtually all assets passed from one generation to the next should go into Dynasty Trusts.

"[Estate taxes are not really taxes but] penalties imposed on those who neglect to plan ahead or who retain unskilled estate planners." – Henry Aaron and Alicia Munnell

B. Family Limited Partnership (FLP): Giving Away Much More than $5 Million – "Discounting"

A Family Limited Partnership (FLP) is an entity that you can create for a family business, rental property, or other actively managed assets. It offers many management and asset protection benefits. It also creates opportunities for the transfer of family wealth to the next generation in a tax wise manner.

There are two types of partners in a FLP. There is the "general partner," who has control of the partnership. There are also the "limited partners," who have no control.

A properly structured FLP allows you to "discount" the value of assets that are transferred from you, the owner of the assets, to your children and grandchildren. This well-established approach therefore allows you to leverage both the $14,000 annual exclusion and the $5 million lifetime gifting opportunity to substantially higher levels.

1. <u>How does discounting work</u>? If you own a portion of an asset but have no control over it, its value is obviously limited. You may need cash and

want to sell the asset, but you cannot do so. It is not your choice, and it is not within your power.

Alternatively, you may have control of an asset and give a partial interest to one of your children. If you kept complete control, the value of the interests owned by your children is limited and compromised. Your children are powerless. They can neither access, nor benefit from, their limited interest unless you cooperate. This is why tax law allows you to discount the value of an interest in a limited partnership.

Example 9-3: Give up control, keep income

Assume that you place rental property valued at $1 million in a FLP. You transfer a 1% interest to your daughter. You keep a 99% interest, which means that you will retain virtually all of the net income. You name your daughter as the general partner. She therefore has complete management and control of the FLP asset. At the time of your passing, a discount of perhaps 35% to 45% can typically be taken. While the market value of 99% of the FLP assets may approach $1 million, a 40% discount means that the value *for estate tax purposes* is only $600,000. In this hypothetical example, some $160,000 in estate tax is avoided.

A discount is allowed because you have given up complete control of the partnership and, therefore, the underlying assets. You did not have the power, for example, to decide about capital improvements or when to sell the property. Only your daughter, the general partner, has this power. The value of this asset in your estate is therefore substantially compromised and reduced.

Example 9-4: Give up ownership but keep control

You devoted your life to a business that is now successful and valued at $5 million. Your son works in the business and is the likely successor. Because you have a large estate, this $5 million asset will generate an estate tax of $2 million. You create a FLP and transfer ownership of the business into the FLP.

You want to remove this valuable asset from your estate, but you also want to retain control -- for at least five more years. You will name yourself as the general partner and your son as the limited partner. You immediately begin transferring limited partnership interests to your son.

Because your son is a limited partner, he has no control of the partnership assets. Moreover, his limited partnership interest is virtually unmarketable. Who would buy a portion of the family partnership when you are still in complete control? To attract any independent buyer, the value of any interest would have to be very substantially reduced. For these and other reasons, the value of any transferred interest is substantially discounted.

Example 9-5: Use the $14,000 annual exclusion to leverage the transfer of partnership assets

Rather than transfer partnership units valued at $14,000 to your son, you instead transferred $23,000 worth of partnership assets and discount the value by 40%. The value of this transfer is therefore $13,800. Because it is less than the annual exclusion, it is not reportable to the IRS. Also, it does not affect or diminish your lifetime estate tax protection.

Example 9-6: Use the current $5 million giving opportunity to transfer partnership units

You can transfer 99% of the partnership units, valued at $4,950,000, to your son as the limited partner. If a 40% discount is allowed, $1,980,000 worth of the partnership effectively disappears for transfer tax purposes. After the discount, the value of this gift is only $2,970,000. This gift is reported on a federal gift tax return, Form 709. You thereby exhausted more than half of your $5 million gift and estate tax protection. The benefit: you avoided some $800,000 in estate tax, at minimum. You also transferred effective ownership of the partnership at its current appraised value. If the business grows in value in the future, 99% of the growth is in your son's estate, rather than yours. It therefore avoids estate tax exposure at the time of your death.

2. How was the size of the discount determined? An independent professional, such as a CPA, reviews the partnership agreement. The size of

the discount is based on the specific elements or provisions of the partnership agreement. Criteria relied upon by the IRS to determine the size of the discount are no secret. The independent professional produces a written, detailed appraisal of the partnership and proffers the size of the discount that can legitimately be taken.

In the context of FLPs – or virtually all transfers – shares or interests are best transferred into *Dynasty or Family Protection Trusts for the benefit of a child, children, or grandchildren.* In this way, asset protection benefits are captured and all or most of the value of transferred interests are protected from estate tax exposure on the passing of your children. See Chapter 8 for a complete discussion of Dynasty Trusts.

C. Limited Liability Corporation (LLC)

A Limited Liability Corporation (LLC) is conceptually similar to the Family Limited Partnership in that it, too, allows for the discounting of interests when properly structured.

The LLC is often utilized for asset protection purposes. It is designed, quite literally, to limit your liability in the event that litigation focuses on an asset within the LLC. Limited Liability Corporation shares or interests can be transferred with similar discounting opportunities.

D. Fractional Shares of Real Property

If you own an entire interest in real property, it is obvious that the entire value is in your estate at the time of your passing. What if you only own a 90% interest? If the market value of the property is $1 million, is your interest valued at $900,000 for estate tax purposes?

No. If you do not own an entire interest, your control and your ability to take such steps as refinancing or selling the property is compromised. As a result, you can typically take a 15% to 30%[1] discount when determining the value of your interest for estate tax purposes.

Example 9-7: Fractional share and discounting

You transfer a 10% interest in your $10 million rental property to your daughter's Family Protection Trust for her benefit. The 90% interest you retained would be valued at $9 million if only market value is considered. The limitations that flow from owning only a fractional share – anything less than 100% – may allow your estate to discount your interest by perhaps 25% at the time of your passing. After the discount is taken, the value of this interest is reduced to only $6,750,000, removing $2,250,000 from your taxable estate. Over $900,000 in estate taxes are thereby avoided.

Caveat: Implementation of this approach is more complicated than the simple transfer of a fractional share interest to one or more others – or to their Family Protection Trusts. Documentation and

---

[1] The reader is again reminded that examples are simplified for understanding. Although estimates of discounting are generally accurate, no effort is made to provide either a detailed analysis or precise numbers. My goal is to convey the concept, not the details.

agreements must address such issues as the "partition action," which allows a partial owner to effectively force the sale of the property.

E. Residence Trust

Your home may be your most valuable asset. It may be valued from $900,000 to $5,000,000. You may also have a vacation home with comparable value. If these assets are in your estate at the time of your passing, they alone can generate an enormous estate tax liability.

The Grantor Retained Interest Trust (GRIT) is an irrevocable trust into which you transfer your home as a means of transferring ownership to your children or, as always recommended, to Family Protection or Dynasty Trusts established for their benefit. This approach is utilized because it enables you to significantly "discount" the value of the transferred residence.

Variations are also known as Personal Residence Trusts (PRTs) and Qualified Personal Residence Trusts (QPRTs).

<u>Example 9-8: Protecting the Residence</u>

You have a residence valued at $2 million. You have other assets and you have a taxable estate. If you own the residence at the time of your passing, by which time it has increased in value to $4 million, it will generate an estate tax in excess of $1.6 million. You instead transfer the property into this irrevocable trust, the PRT. The trust provides that you will retain effective control and use of the property for a designated number of years, perhaps 10. At the end of the 10 year period, the trust terminates and the property is distributed to the Dynasty Trusts established for the benefit of your children. At that point, while you are still living, your children's trusts become the owners of the property. The property is removed from your estate.

What is the value of the gift of this $4 million residence? Because your children have to wait 10 years before they obtain ownership, the gift is not worth even $2 million at the time you transfer it into the trust. At that point in time, they have an expectancy or a future interest and nothing more. Because of this delay, the value of the gift at the time it is made is discounted by approximately 50%. The size of the discount depends primarily on the length of the term. The longer the term, the bigger the discount because the recipients have to wait a longer period of time before they obtain ownership. The shorter the term, the smaller the discount because they will obtain ownership sooner.

In the above example, you may wind up giving away a house ultimately valued at $4 million, though it is treated as a gift of only $1 million. The technique makes $3 million disappear, saving $1,200,000 in estate taxes.

Consider this analogy: If you give a one dollar bill to your son, he takes it and can immediately spend it. This is a completed gift valued at $1. If you instead placed the one dollar bill in a sealed envelope and set it aside for your son, but provide that he does not get it for 10 years, the current value of the gift is substantially less than one dollar. Would your son not rather get $.50 right now rather than wait 10 years to get a $1 bill? Put differently, the current value of the one dollar gift that the recipient will not get for 10 years is worth much less than $1 to the recipient when the envelope is opened.

Similarly, the PRT or QPRT is the sealed envelope. The irrevocable trust holds title to the property until a term of years expires. Only then do the recipients get the property.

This trust can also be used for a second residence. A vacation home can therefore be transferred into such a trust, with the same discount benefits. This same technique may also be applied to gifts of other types of assets if the beneficiary(ies) of the trust are not lineal descendants. Such trusts can be used to tremendous advantage to shelter gifts to nieces, nephews, and other family members.

F. Intentionally Defective Irrevocable Trust (IDIT)

An IDIT is an irrevocable trust. It is also a "grantor trust," which means that the person establishing the trust, the grantor, must pay income taxes on the income created by the trust. However, the assets in the trust are not includable in the grantor's estate for estate tax purposes.

Here's how it works: a grantor will typically make a small gift to an IDIT with cash or property. The IDIT then buys a valuable asset from the grantor, using the relatively modest amount of money in the trust as a "down payment," covering the rest of the value through a promissory note. Through this transfer, the grantor has "frozen" the value of the asset and has transferred wealth by converting an asset increasing in value into an asset with a fixed yield, such as an interest-bearing note. The IDIT shifts all increase in value above the comparatively low fixed yield out of the grantor (parent's) estate to the trust beneficiaries (children) without gift or estate tax.

The grantor can also discount the value of the asset transferred into the IDIT, for reasons discussed in prior sections. This reduces the fair market value of the asset, as well as the value of the promissory note, often dramatically reducing the amount subject to estate and gift tax.

G. Charitable Trust & Charitable Giving

Those who are philanthropically inclined – and many who are not – take advantage of tax-wise planning opportunities to favor charitable giving.

Most of us have issues that concern us deeply. Because of family experiences, we may want to support cancer, Parkinson's, autism, or other forms of medical research. We may want to support individuals with such diagnoses and family caregivers. We may want to support educational institutions that gave us our entry to the world of economic security or that expanded our horizons.

Whatever the cause, we may want to leave a portion of our estate to address these issues and achieve certain goals, particularly if doing so will offer tax advantages.

Upon your passing, any amount of money can be left to a tax exempt organization without exposure to estate tax. One of the simplest approaches to eliminate the estate tax is to leave the maximum number of dollars to one's family that can be distributed to them without tax exposure, with the balance going to one or more tax exempt organizations. If an individual passed in 2013 and the estate is valued at $7,250,000, $5,250,000 would go to favored individuals, with $2 million going to the favored tax exempt entity. With relative simplicity, estate tax is eliminated.

However, for most individuals, it is far more complicated. They want to capture benefits for themselves or their children, while simultaneously supporting favored tax exempt organizations. This is typically achieved by creating and funding appropriately drafted trusts.

A Charitable Trust is an irrevocable trust designed to reduce taxes while benefiting a charity. These trusts are attractive if you also have charitable giving inclinations, although many individuals create and utilize this trust approach exclusively for tax planning and income purposes.

There are two main types of Charitable Trusts: the Charitable Remainder Trust (CRT) and the Charitable Lead Trust (CLT). Both are discussed below. See also the discussion of Family Foundations and Donor Advised funds, below.

1. Charitable Remainder Trust (CRT)

Assets are placed in a CRT for a specified time period. During that time period, the beneficiaries, such as your children, receive a certain amount of income. At the end of the time period, the remainder of the trust is donated to the designated charity. The income to your children can be calculated by a percentage of the trust principal, as in the case of the Charitable Remainder Unitrust (CRUT). Alternately, your children can receive a fixed dollar amount each year, as in the Charitable Remainder Annuity Trust (CRAT).

a. Charitable Remainder Unitrust (CRUT)

This approach is particularly appropriate if you have a valuable asset, say a rental property or founders' stock, with low cost basis that is insufficiently productive. You may want to generate more income from the asset by reinvesting the value, but sale of the asset would generate a punishing capital gains tax. This trust allows for the sale of the property without exposure to capital gains tax and the guarantee of lifetime income.

Example 9-9: CRUT increases income, captures income tax benefit

You own a four-plex valued at $1.2 million. The cost basis is only $200,000. If you sell the property, you will have a $1 million capital gain. The federal capital gains tax is 20%. California is one of many states that add its own capital gains tax, which approaches 10%. Approximately $300,000, or 30% of the capital gain, is therefore lost to capital gains tax exposure. Net proceeds of sale after other costs are reduced to only $900,000. The substantially reduced net proceeds are then invested to give you an income stream. If those assets are invested and you achieve a 4% rate of return, you will have annual income of $36,000, all of which is exposed to income tax.

If you instead establish a CRUT, which is an irrevocable trust, you transfer title of the property into the trust. The trustee then sells the property. Because assets remaining in the trust at the time of your death go to a tax-exempt organization, such as a university, hospital, or your other favorite charity, *capital gains taxes are avoided*. If the net proceeds are therefore $1.1 million, the trust can provide that you are to receive a 4% return for the rest of your life. This will give you $44,000 per year, an increase of $8,000 per year. If the underlying value of the trust assets increases, your annual income increases because you are guaranteed 4% of the annual value of trust assets. Also beneficial is the fact that income from this trust will enjoy protection from income tax exposure for a number of years because the transfer of this asset into the charitable trust generates a significant income tax deduction that can be used to offset income in the current year and up to five following years.

Over a 10-year period, an extra $80,000 is received as income, much of which is protected from income tax exposure.

b. Charitable Remainder Annuity Trust (CRAT)

You may prefer an annuity approach, which guarantees you a certain number of dollars every year, regardless of growth or decrease in the value of the underlying trust assets. This is to be compared with the Charitable Remainder Unitrust (CRUT), where annual income could decrease if the value of invested assets decreases. The annuity approach is more conservative and more reliable, and is particularly suitable for seniors.

2. Charitable Lead Trust

A Charitable Lead Trust can also be used to transfer assets to children or others at a significantly reduced tax liability. The trust makes a fixed "annuity" payment or a variable "unitrust" payment to a charity for a specified term. After the term ends, the assets are either returned to you or are passed on to children or other loved ones. If passed on to heirs, the estate or gift taxes on the value of the gift are reduced or eliminated.

Example 9-10: Charitable giving and discounting

You transfer $1,000,000 into a twenty-year charitable lead trust to benefit your favorite charity. The charity receives $50,000 in income annually for the purposes specified by you. At the end of the twenty-year term, your two children receive the trust principal.

For gift tax purposes, only the present value of the "remainder," or the amount your children will ultimately receive, is subject to tax. Treasury tables project the value of the remainder to be about $213,000. Assuming a 6% annual return, and after the annual distributions to the charity, at the end of the twenty-year term the trust principal has grown to about $1,280,500. Your children receive the entire $1,280,500, while your gift tax liability is limited to $213,000. In this case, you have ultimately made a tax-free gift to your children of $1,067,300.

*   *   *

3. Replace Donated Family Wealth with an Irrevocable Life Insurance Trust (ILIT)

A properly structured CRT generates a substantially increased income, much of which is protected from income tax exposure. If you would like to replace the wealth that is ultimately transferred to the charity through the CRT rather than passing to your children, you can use a portion of your substantially increased annual income and invest it in a life insurance policy through an Irrevocable Life Insurance Trust (ILIT).

Example 9-11: Charitable giving and wealth replacement

You transfer $20,000 of your increased annual income to an ILIT, as described earlier in this chapter. The ILIT uses those funds to purchase a $1 million life insurance policy. Upon your passing, the full $1 million passes to

Dynasty Trusts established for the benefit of your children.

By using an irrevocable life insurance trust and life insurance, all of the following advantages may be captured:

1. Transfer of appreciated assets without exposure to capital gains tax.

2. Transfer of assets with minimal or no exposure to gift or estate tax.

3. Joy and satisfaction of supporting a favored tax exempt organization.

4. Purchasing life insurance in an ILIT so that children or other heirs ultimately receive a significant distribution typically as valuable as the gifted assets, notwithstanding the charitable gift.

There are many reasons why individuals decide to make charitable gifts. When done in a sophisticated manner, charitable giving can also reduce estate tax exposure, often without reducing the size of inherited assets.

Be a hero to your favorite charity: If you establish a charitable trust, be sure to inform the charity that is the ultimate beneficiary. They will honor you, invite you to dinners, and generally fete you. Enjoy it!

H. Family Foundation and Donor Advised Fund

In conjunction with a CRT or independently, you can create a Family Foundation and transfer unlimited assets into the Foundation to remove them from your taxable estate. You can transfer assets into a Family Foundation while you are living or upon your passing. Either way, the assets avoid estate tax. Lifetime gifts can also generate income tax deductions.

When you create the Foundation, you identify its charitable objectives. Your family members can be officers and directors of the Foundation. They may be employed by the Foundation. To many, this is a means by which family wealth can be enjoyed by future generations in a meaningful way.

Still another option – in the world of charitable giving – is a gift to a Donor Advised Fund. Such funds are maintained and managed most typically by Community Foundations.

For example, the Gold family transfers $500,000 to its local Community Foundation to establish the Gold Fund to support open space and the arts. The Gold Fund is to exist in perpetuity, with annually earned interest distributed to appropriate tax exempt entities to support its work. Gold family members advise The Foundation staff and board about how or to which entities annual distributions are to be made. Someday, grandchildren will become the sources of advice.

Community Foundations presumptively respect the advice of family members, allowing investment without the cost and other challenges inherent in establishing a Family Foundation.

I. Grantor Retained Annuity Trust (GRAT)

The Grantor Retained Annuity Trust (GRAT) is an irrevocable trust into which you put assets for a certain term of years. You receive an annuity, or fixed income stream, during that term. When the term is completed, the remaining assets are distributed tax-free to children or other beneficiaries or held in a trust for their benefit. After the expiration of the term, the remaining assets are not part of your estate for estate tax purposes.

The GRAT allows the grantor to leverage transfers to children and shift all appreciation above a relatively low presumed rate of return. As long as the asset in the GRAT increases in value more than the presumed rate, the children win.

The value of the gift for gift tax purposes is the value of the property transferred to it, minus the value of the grantor's retained annuity interest. The annuity, or fixed income stream, is a fixed percentage of the initial contribution and, therefore, is a fixed dollar amount. Current historically low interest rates make this approach exceptionally interesting. This type of trust is especially useful if you put in assets that you expect will substantially increase in value in the near future.

Example 9-12: Retaining income, delayed transfer to children

In July 2009, Mrs. S transfers $1 million into a GRAT. The federal rate for determining the present value of an annuity that month was 2.8% per year. Given the federal tax rules on GRATs, the yearly annuity payment to Mrs. S is set at $116,038 for a term of ten years.

If the assets in the GRAT have a low growth rate equal to the federal tax rate of 2.8% per year, there would not be much benefit to using a GRAT. This is because the required annuity distributions to Mrs. S would eliminate any long-term growth in the GRAT. However, if the assets in the GRAT instead appreciated at 8%, approximately a half million dollars would be passed along to the remainder beneficiaries with no tax exposure.

If the GRAT assets consistently grow faster than the federal tax rate, the GRAT will have a larger remainder to pass to the beneficiaries. This is why GRATs are most beneficial when federal tax rates are low, as now, and the GRAT contains highly appreciating assets.

J. Individual Retirement Accounts (IRAs) and Other Retirement Accounts

You may have significant assets in a retirement account and enjoy deferred income taxation exposure. These assets are part of your taxable estate. They present significant challenges in the context of estate tax avoidance.

If you are charitably inclined, these assets are ideal for ultimate distribution to your favorite tax exempt organization. Individuals with large, taxable estates can *lose up to 80%* of the value of retirement accounts. This is because their value is exposed to estate tax, currently 40%. A $1 million IRA in a taxable estate will therefore generate estate tax exposure as high as $400,000. Moreover, IRA funds are exposed to income tax as they are distributed. Those exposed to higher marginal income tax rates can lose over 35% of that income to income tax exposure.

Highly motivated individuals sometimes withdraw significant portions of or all retirement assets and accept the income tax exposure. They then take tax planning steps, outlined above, to protect the value of assets remaining after income tax is paid.

Example 9-13: $500,000 IRA and estate tax

Mr. White has a large, taxable estate. It includes a $500,000 IRA. His annual income is relatively modest, in part because he has invested in tax-free municipal bonds. Over the course of two years, he withdraws 100% of his IRA money. His effective income tax rate is 33%, so $166,667 is paid in income tax as a result of the IRA distributions. He then has $333,333 in his name. He can invest those assets in real property and utilize a Family Limited Partnership, Limited Liability Corporation, or some other entity to substantially reduce his estate tax exposure.

If he has a *Roth IRA*, other opportunities

present themselves since distributions are not subject to income tax. He would, nevertheless, hesitate to withdraw all funds because of the beneficial tax treatment that can be passed along to future generations.

K. "Disclaiming" Inherited Assets

> *"If more people knew about the benefits of a disclaimer, its use would skyrocket." – M.G.*

A radically underused, yet very powerful tax planning tool is a "disclaimer." It is an option that presents itself whenever an individual is inheriting assets. It is a way of saying "No, thank you" to all or any part of an inheritance. If an inheritance is disclaimed, it passes as if the person disclaiming the assets were already deceased. While it may seem illogical or even incredible to reject an inheritance, it can make sense in many situations.

Most typically, a disclaimer should be considered when an individual already has a taxable estate and is about to inherit assets. The inherited assets will add to the taxable estate, exposing over half of those assets to estate tax at the time of death. The disclaimed assets will likely pass to this person's children, so they remain in the family.

Example 9-14: Rejecting an inheritance and avoiding tax

Mrs. Smith is a widow, 70 years of age, and has an estate valued at $6 million. She is very tax sensitive. She learns that her aunt died and is leaving her an inheritance of

$1,000,000. If she accepts the inheritance, her estate grows by $1,000,000. Her estate tax exposure also grows by $1 million, adding over $400,000 in potential tax liability.

Mrs. Smith decides to "disclaim" the inheritance. Her aunt's trust provided that, if Mrs. Smith predeceased her aunt, the inheritance would instead go to Mrs. Smith's two children. As a result, the $1 million passes directly to Mrs. Smith's two children in equal shares. The $1 million therefore avoids estate tax exposure at Mrs. Smith's passing. Some $400,000 in tax is thereby saved and her children enjoy immediate use of the money.

L. Other Planning Opportunities Exist

We make no effort in this publication to identify every conceivable approach to address estate tax exposure. Nor can we identify which approach is appropriate for any given individual. Many variables that complicate every real life situation must be taken into account when planning to avoid estate tax. The challenge and the opportunity are to implement a plan that is consistent with your values and your goals as an individual and as a family.

Chapter 10: Values, Motivation, and the Impact of Inherited Wealth
The "Trust Baby" Syndrome

Is there a point at which you have too much wealth – to a point where you worry about its impact on your children? Might it affect their motivation, quality of life, and values?

For the "mega wealthy," this is an inevitable concern. For those with comfortable estates, it is a worry that also rewards attention.

A. Defining Wealth – At What Point Do You Worry? At What Point Do You Address This Issue?

"Wealth" is an elusive term that defies simple definition. Is it your net worth on a balance sheet? Is it your liquid assets, setting aside your residence? Is it a state of mind?

I have found that, for individuals, "wealth" is a remarkably self-defining term. For some, accumulation of a certain amount achieves wealth status. It could be $3 million, $8 million, $12 million, or more. For most, a fascinating pattern emerges. Many formal studies show that wealth is a highly relative term. For those with objectively larger estates – perhaps exceeding $3 million – real wealth is defined as *"double whatever I have."*

B. Protecting Wealth and Family Values

In this book, two approaches are pursued. First, we consistently focus on the preservation of family wealth by professional, sophisticated planning. Second, we have a multigenerational planning focus. With good planning, we can protect assets from tax, litigation, and divorce for multiple generations. This is the easy part. More challenging is the need to do so while simultaneously preserving individual motivation and family values.

1. What Are the Worries?

Worries about the impact of family wealth include the following:

- Lack of motivation – "Trust Babies" or "Trustofarians."

- Drug and alcohol abuse; other self-destructive behavior.

- Thrill-seeking and dangerous, risky behavior.

- Lack of self-confidence and diminished evaluation of "self-worth."

- Difficulty forming close relationships.

2. What Are the Benefits of Wealth?

While we urge wealthy families to be attentive to problems that can arise, we acknowledge and elevate the many benefits.

- At the most basic level, having sufficient assets so your children can purchase homes. This is particularly important for those who live in communities where housing is extraordinarily expensive.

- Financial security to the point where daily, erosive money worries are minimized or eliminated.

- The opportunity to seek and obtain higher levels of education and experience.

- The opportunity to pursue higher values for one's self, one's family, and one's community.

- The opportunity to pursue philanthropic activities.

- The gift of time – to maximize one's potential.

- Comfort knowing that the grandchildren and great-grandchildren will not face economic hardship.

- Enhanced likelihood that children and grandchildren will have greater educational and employment opportunities.

None of these benefits are automatically achieved. They require work, time, and living lives that are consistent with the values you want your children to absorb.

C. Should You Tell Your Child What You Have?

This is a tough one. Those with significant assets worry about the impact of inherited wealth on a child's motivation and life values. They worry about potential harm that can be done by inherited wealth as they simultaneously enjoy the possibility of giving their children lives that can be enhanced and enriched.

I have counseled countless people with substantial estates. I have represented and worked with countless individuals who directly inherited wealth or who were beneficiaries of trusts established by wealthy parents or grandparents. While I am careful not to generalize excessively, some lessons have been learned.

The question, then, is if you should or should not tell your children what you have. The answer is a very unsatisfying, "It depends." The real question: On what does it depend?

1. The Benefits of Sharing

You may have a business that you want to keep in the family. If this be the case, your children or the child most likely to maintain the business must become involved with the business, understand its economics, and therefore develop a sense of its value. Inevitably, this will lead to an understanding of the overall size of the estate.

Your planning will inevitably include the establishment of trusts, family partnerships, or other entities. While you will be the initial trustee or general partner in such entities, there will come a time when you will no longer be able to serve in this capacity. It is prudent, if not necessary, to educate the child or children who are to take responsibility for trust and partnership management about what these responsibilities entail while you are able and healthy. If such responsibilities are thrust upon them when they are unprepared and relatively ignorant about them, and when you may be in a health crisis, the challenges are obvious.

It is necessary to educate the next generation about your assets and business when there is a diagnosis of a debilitating condition – physiological or mental – that will result in your inability to manage your estate. Most starkly, your child may be designated to take over management of your estate upon your passing. Again, it is far better to educate children about these responsibilities well in advance rather than in a crisis context.

> **Preparing Your Child as Your Successor Trustee**
> We strongly recommend that the child chosen to be your successor trustee be educated about your trusts and estate planning in general, and your chosen approach, in particular. We recommend that you include this child in meetings with your estate planning attorney. We recommend that you take steps to educate your chosen successor trustee (child) about the operation of an AB Trust, a Dynasty Trust, a Family Limited Partnership if you have one, and any other entities you have created.

2. Good Reasons to Share the Information

Particularly if your child or children are reliable and mature, it can be very wise and helpful to tell them about the size of the estate that they will inherit. This will help them define and understand their own future.

It is also an opportunity to test them. Once they know about wealth that they will inherit or may have already inherited in trust, are they affected? Do they somehow become less responsible or less focused in their lives or work? Is their work ethic somehow diminished? Or do they work harder and learn more to be better prepared?

Armed with this information, do they take steps to learn about tax, money management, and other such topics that will be part of their lives?

You may be implementing a tax and asset preservation plan to preserve the family business or other family assets. Educating your children about such steps and involving them may be an absolute necessity.

3. The Downside of Not Telling Your Children

As you think about your children's understanding of your wealth, realize that they are neither blind nor ignorant. They observe your lifestyle. They know where you live. They have some sense of your wealth. The expectation of inherited wealth will affect them, whether you like it or not.

A worry is that the imagination can create illusions about wealth. They may think you have much more than you do. They may expect to inherit everything, though you plan on leaving them only a portion of the estate.

They may, on the other hand, be unaware of a potentially comfortable inheritance. They may make unhealthy or unwise decisions that compromise personal growth. This may be an outcome that you abhor.

For example, they may choose to live in an area with lower cost housing, poorer schools, and less opportunity for themselves and their children.

If they feel economically challenged, they may not obtain that specialist or counselor that is needed for a troubled child.

They may not obtain the healthcare or other personal services that they need to have better, more productive lives.

They may not travel to family and holiday events because of concerns about cost.

D. Can You Leave Them Too Much?

1. The "Trust Baby" Syndrome is Real

We have observed many individuals who are supported by trusts established by parents or grandparents for their well-being. Particularly when such trusts hold ample assets, the child or grandchild (the beneficiary) is relieved of the need to work and earn a living, for better or worse.

The fact is that some inheritors are troubled and adversely affected by inherited wealth. Some have no motivation and drift through life. Some go to college and obtain training and degrees in the arts, pursuing no path to economic viability. Consciously or unconsciously, they conclude that they should prepare themselves for the finer things in life, that they should avoid menial or unstimulating work.

Such inheritors may avoid real work, developing no sense of personal responsibility and initiative.

Thankfully such outcomes are not typical. Inherited wealth is more typically a wonderful thing, allowing one's family members to achieve remarkable success and to contribute incomparable value to their communities.

Yet, the phenomenon is sufficiently real and rewards attention.

2. What Do You Do About the Trust Baby Syndrome?

Busy, successful parents typically want to spend "quality time" with their children. This is appropriately defined as time for play, vacations, and other enjoyable behavior. It requires focus and resolve to also – and purposefully – have time with children that is designed to create and reinforce work ethic, positive family values, and community responsibility.

There must be an awareness of potential problems before a strategy or approach can be developed. Elements of a lifelong family approach can take many forms.

a. Practice Frugality. Warren Buffett continues to live in his simple family home in Omaha, Nebraska. He does not live in a multimillion dollar mansion. Many say that he is the inspiration to Middle America. Conversely, profligacy offers a dangerous example to the next generation.

b. Learn Money Management. Children will more clearly understand the value and limits of money if they actually manage it. Budgeting and balancing a checkbook are perhaps the most obvious skills to acquire.

c. Communication, Involvement, and Engagement. Consuming devotion to work, and perhaps to the country club, leaves little opportunity for family communication and values development. Children can be left in a relative vacuum. They will be predominantly influenced by their peers and the media. This may not be an ideal scenario.

Involvement in one's community, including a church or synagogue, is typically a positive influence. Engagement on important political and social issues can be as important.

d. Understanding and celebrating family legacy. Many studies show that knowledge of one's heritage or legacy increases a sense of personal worth and the development of positive values. Many families therefore take extraordinary steps to acquaint their children with the difficulties, challenges, and successes of grandparents and great-grandparents.

e. Be careful about "pursuing your passion." Perhaps because we did not do so, because Mr. Rogers taught all of our kids that they are special, or because we believe that all of our children are above average, many parents have convinced our children that they should not pursue unrewarding career paths – just for the money. We want our children to develop to their full potential. It is no coincidence that an extraordinary percentage of our children – children of baby boomers – pursue careers in filmmaking, acting, costume design, screen writing, dance, and other related fields of art and creativity. One estimate is that there are 1,000 young people seeking every real job in Hollywood's film industry. The result can be high levels of frustration, despondency, and unemployment. Transition to a "real job" becomes difficult.

Perhaps less emphasis should be placed on the pursuit of one's passion than on development of balanced, comprehensively educated children who can engage positively with the business community (put bluntly, "get a job") so that they can pursue their passions as avocations. Perhaps this will create more balanced individuals who are more able to engage productively and happily in the real world.

f. <u>Family Discussions; Family Mission Statement</u>. Some families develop "family mission statements" or "family value statements." This approach was strongly reinforced by the writings of Stephen Covey in his *Seven Habits* book and series. Family retreats and family discussions can be invaluable and offer a sense of shared direction.

The following is a Mission Statement developed by one California family:

"We provide a concrete and emotional safe haven for each other. Each of us knows we are loved, accepted, and can seek a caring ear and a helping hand. We consciously enjoy each other as we share pleasurable experiences and during those "mundane" moments of family life. Our family's default is warmth and friendliness."

g. <u>Family Counseling</u>. The perfect family – where everyone gets along and communication is robust, open, and positive – is a rarity. If communication becomes impossible, there is a role for professional counseling.

h. <u>Philanthropic Involvement</u>. This can take the form of personal, hands-on volunteer work with local causes. It can take the form of active participation on the board of a family foundation or family advice fund through a community foundation. It can take the form of financial support for nonprofit organizations, ideally after family discussions about choices.

Countless articles and books are devoted to this challenging topic that we address too briefly in this publication. The brevity of this treatment must not, in the reader, suggest a minimized level of concern. We see this as a very emotional, challenging, and important topic.

Words of an Inheritor

A young woman was interviewed by authors of <u>The Legacy of Inherited Wealth: Interviews with Heirs</u> (Blouin Editor, 1995). She defined herself as an "ungrounded person."

"Affluence permitted me to become even more ungrounded... Having so much money added to my sense of groundlessness and contradiction. I was alienated from the simple business of ordinary life. I felt no necessity to do anything... then I felt that I had nothing to look forward to."

To deal with her deeply conflicted emotions, she took a job as a janitor in a shopping mall and lived on that meager income, a process that gave her much of the grounding that she needed.

E. Community Involvement and Personal Values Development

Wealth and creature comforts can give us and our families a false sense of security. We may feel insulated from crime, health crisis, and physical labor.

The fact is, however, that we live in a broader, wider community over which we have little control. If our community is unsafe, we are unsafe. If members of our community are not well-educated, quality of life inevitably erodes.

Accepting responsibility for quality of life by civic involvement, volunteerism, and providing financial support for service organizations are, therefore, profoundly in our self-interest. If our children and grandchildren observe us exercising such responsibility, they will follow. Social scientists and political scientists agree: participation and acts of community involvement are as important to values development in the next generation as they are to our own health and well-being.

F. Estate Planning Steps to Address Heir Dependency

In estate planning, address this concern directly. Parents who are concerned about financial dependency may include "incentive" provisions in a trust established for a child or grandchild.

For example, a trust may limit distributions for the beneficiary's health and basic housing. It could allow additional distributions only if the beneficiary works. A dollar may be distributed to the beneficiary only if the beneficiary earns a dollar by employment.

Countless variations on this theme exist. A trust can be drafted with great creativity, responding to individual needs and circumstances.

Chapter 11: Take Action! Protect Your Estate!

"You are on the right track, but you'll get run over if you don't get up." -- Will Rogers

First, objectively <u>determine the size of your estate</u>. If you did not yet do so, use the "Valuing Your Estate" exercise in Chapter 2. For this exercise, do not use conservative figures. If anything, be optimistic about values. Remember that assets are professionally appraised at the time of your passing. The IRS may audit your estate and challenge values that appear to be artificially low.

Based on the size of your estate, you can easily <u>calculate your estate tax exposure</u>. If you are single, remember that everything over $5,250,000 will be exposed to estate tax. If you are a couple, your revocable trust will protect $10,500,000.

<u>Realize that current gifting legislation presents an opportunity</u>. If you are a married couple, you can give away up to $10,500,000 million this year without paying any tax whatsoever. Moreover, the recipients will pay no tax as a result of the transfer. By using discounting techniques, you can leverage this opportunity and give away $18 million or more. You may decide to make significant gifts to Dynasty Trusts for your children to "lock in" this historic wealth transfer opportunity.

Even if you do not now have a taxable estate, your estate may grow or the tax laws could change and become less advantageous.

Aside from tax, you may have special, possibly difficult family circumstances that must not be ignored and that can be addressed in estate planning to protect your children.

Consult with an experienced tax and estate planning attorney. Only in this way will you be able to identify the planning options that are appropriate for you. You are unique and your plan must be crafted to both reflect and respect your values and your goals. It may include a Family Limited Partnership and the Charitable Remainder Trust. It may include a Personal Residence Trust and fractional share giving. It may include an Irrevocable Life Insurance Trust. It may include a Special Needs Trust. It may include all or none of these approaches.

It must effectively and efficiently reduce or eliminate your estate tax exposure in a way that is appropriate for you and your situation.

9 Step Estate Tax Avoidance Checklist

STEP 1: Estimate size of your estate
See Chart B in Chapter 2.

STEP 2: Estimate estate tax exposure – as of 2013.
Single: 40% of everything over $5.25 million
Married: 40% of everything over $10.5 million

STEP 3: Recover from shock. Take deep breaths. Resolve to act to avoid estate tax.

STEP 4: Use Dynasty Trusts for children's inheritance and/or gifts.

STEP 5: Consider the need for trust planning to address challenging or problematic circumstances in the family. Review *Your Revocable Trust is Not "One Size Fits All"* in Chapter 4.

STEP 6: Review Chapter 9 – summary of tax planning options.

STEP 7: Obtain professional advice to identify best options for you.

STEP 8: Implement the estate planning and tax avoidance plan of choice.

STEP 9: CELEBRATE!

"Implement a tax avoidance plan that is right for you. No heads in the sand!" -- M.G.

Contact us at Gilfix & La Poll Associates, LLP
2300 Geng Road, Suite 200
Palo Alto, California 94303
Toll Free 1-800-244-9424
650-493-8070
www.Gilfix.com

Chapter 12: How We Take Care of Our Client Community
The Gilfix & La Poll Peace of Mind Program

In the office of Gilfix & La Poll, we offer trust clients participation in our Peace of Mind Program. For a modest cost, our clients are given unlimited opportunities to ask questions about their trusts and to have them effectively monitored and maintained. Integral to this approach are two free services that very effectively bring the child into the circle of planning and educate the child about the operation and management of these trusts.

✓ *Free annual meeting*: Members of this Peace of Mind Program are given a free annual meeting to review their planning and to identify developments that will reward attention. Clients are encouraged to bring their successor trustees so their successor trustees can learn about the approach and ask questions about their future responsibilities. Clients are encouraged to bring their children, whether or not they are the successor trustees.

✓ Members of the Peace of Mind Program are offered a *series of free seminars* designed to educate successor trustees, typically children, about the operation of the parents' trust. These popular seminars also explain dynasty trusts that are typically established for their own benefit. Successor trustees have an opportunity to ask unlimited questions about their future responsibilities and are therefore much better equipped to discharge those responsibilities when the need arises.

There are many other benefits to participation in the Peace of Mind Program. To obtain a complete list, call us at 650-493-8070 or contact us through our website, www.gilfix.com.

Acronyms & Abbreviations

AB Trust – See definition in glossary.

AHCD – Advance Health Care Directive

CLT – Charitable Lead Trust

CRT – Charitable Remainder Trust

CRAT – Charitable Remainder Annuity Trust

CRUT – Charitable Remainder Unitrust

DAPT – Domestic Asset Protection Trust

DPA – Durable Power of Attorney

FLP – Family Limited Partnership

FPT – Family Protection Trust (Dynasty Trust)

GDPA – General Durable Power of Attorney

GST – Generation Skipping Transfer Tax

GRAT – Grantor Retained Annuity Trust

GRIT – Grantor Retained Interest Trust

IDIT – Intentionally Defective Irrevocable Trust

ILIT – Irrevocable Life Insurance Trust

LLC – Limited Liability Company

LLP – Limited Liability Partnership

IRS – Internal Revenue Service

PRT – Personal Residence Trust

QDOT – Qualified Domestic Trust

QPRT – Qualified Personal Residence Trust

RAP – Rule Against Perpetuities

SNT – Special Needs Trust

SSI – Supplemental Security Income

Glossary of Legal Terms in this Book

AB Trust – A type of Revocable Living Trust used by married couples. In this type of living trust, two trusts (trust A and trust B) are created at the time the first spouse dies. By dividing the couple's estate into two trusts at the first death, each spouse can pass the maximum amount of property allowed to avoid federal estate taxes. One trust, usually trust A, is often referred to as the Survivor's Trust or Marital Deduction Trust, and the other trust, usually trust B, is often referred to as the Exemption Trust, Bypass Trust, or Credit Shelter Trust.

Advance Health Care Directive (AHCD) – A document established by an individual (the principal) granting another person (the agent) the right and authority to handle matters related to the health care of the principal.

Annual Exclusion – The amount of property the IRS allows a person to give to another person during a calendar year before a gift tax is assessed and/or a gift tax return must be filed. The amount is increased periodically. There is no limit to the number of people you can give gifts to which qualify for the annual exclusion. To qualify for the annual exclusion, the gift must be one that a recipient can enjoy immediately and over which the recipient will have full control.

Annuity – An investment providing for periodic payment of a definite sum of money, with such payments to continue for life or for a definite number of years.

Asset Protection – Protecting your property from legal problems and taxes during your life and after your death.

Assets – All types of property which can be made available for the payment of debts.

Basis – A tax term, which refers to the original or acquisition value of a property, used to determine the amount of tax that will be assessed if it is sold. The basis is deducted from the sales price of the property when it is sold to determine the profit (capital gain) or loss.

Beneficiary – The person(s) or organization(s) who receive(s) the benefits of trust property held under the terms of a trust.

Bequest – An old legal term meaning a gift or property given under the terms of a will.

Bypass Trust – See Exemption Trust

Charitable Lead Trust (CLT) – An irrevocable trust where a charity receives a certain amount of income during a fixed term. When the term expires, the remainder is distributed to individual beneficiaries, typically family members.

Charitable Remainder Trust (CRT) – An irrevocable trust where individual beneficiaries receive a certain amount of income during a fixed term. When the fixed term expires, the remainder is donated to a charity.

Charitable Remainder Unitrust (CRUT) – A Charitable Remainder Trust where individual beneficiaries receive a fixed percentage (i.e. 4%) of the trust principal each year during the term of the trust.

Charitable Remainder Annuity Trust (CRAT) – A Charitable Remainder Trust where individual beneficiaries receive a fixed dollar amount (i.e. $40,000) each year during the term of the trust.

Charitable Trust – An irrevocable trust having a charitable organization as a lifetime beneficiary (Charitable Lead Trust) or a death beneficiary (Charitable Remainder Trust).

Community Property – Some state laws require that all assets acquired during a marriage belong equally to both spouses, except for gifts and inheritances given specifically to one spouse. The eight states with such laws, including California, are known as community property states.

Consideration – Something which has value, such as real or personal property or a promise given in exchange for another promise.

Credit Shelter Trust – See Exemption Trust

Crummey Trust – An irrevocable trust that allows a limited withdrawal by the trust's beneficiary during a short time period each year. Such trusts qualify for the annual gift tax exclusion. The beneficiary typically does not withdraw the gift during the withdrawal period, and the money remains in the trust until the beneficiary reaches the designated distribution age. Crummey trusts are often used in conjunction with life insurance and Irrevocable Life Insurance Trusts (ILITs).

Decedent – The person who has died.

Death taxes – Taxes levied on the property of a deceased person. Federal death taxes are usually referred to as estate taxes. Local and state death taxes are often referred to as inheritance taxes, or simply death taxes.

Deed – A written document used to evidence ownership and/or transfer title to real estate.

Disclaimer – The refusal of a beneficiary to accept property willed to him. When a disclaimer is made, the property is generally transferred to the person next in line under the will. A disclaimer is also called a renunciation.

Domestic Asset Protection Trust (DAPT) – Such trusts, available in many states, allow an individual to transfer assets into a trust for his own benefit while capturing protection from litigation.

Donor – A person who makes a gift.

Durable Power of Attorney – A document established by an individual (the principal) granting another person (the agent) the right and authority to handle the financial and other affairs of the principal. The Durable Power of Attorney survives through the period of incompetency of the principal.

Dynasty Trust – A trust designed to pass down family wealth for many generations while avoiding transfer taxes (estate tax and generation-skipping tax) to the greatest extent possible. Such trusts typically offer substantial protection in the event of divorce or litigation.

Estate – The aggregate of all assets and debts held (owned) by an individual during his or her life or at the time of his or her death.

Estate Planning – The process by which a person plans for transferring his or her assets at death.

Estate Taxes - Taxes imposed on the "privilege" of transferring property by reason of death. Estate tax is most commonly used in reference to the tax imposed by the Federal Government rather than the state government. Estate taxes are intended to raise revenue for the government and, as a matter of public policy to decrease the likelihood that wealth doesn't concentrate in the hands of a few families.

Exemption Trust – An irrevocable trust that captures the maximum level of estate tax protection for the first spouse to die, holding the assets of that spouse from a married couple's estate. See AB Trust for further explanation.

Family Foundation – An entity into which assets are transferred, removing those assets from your taxable estate. Family members can serve as officers and directors of the foundation, and help to achieve its charitable objectives.

Family Limited Partnership (FLP) – An entity used to hold assets for members of a family. A way to transfer business assets to the next generation at a discounted rate, while retaining control over the assets and/or a right to income.

Family Protection Trust (FPT) – See Dynasty Trust

Generation Skipping Transfer (GST) Tax – A federal tax imposed on large amounts of money given or left to a grandchild or great-grandchild. Its purpose is to keep families from avoiding the estate tax that would be due if the oldest generation left property to their children, who then left it to their children (the original giver's grandchildren).

Generation Skipping Transfer (GST) Trust – See Dynasty Trust

Gift Taxes - Taxes levied by the Federal Government on gifts. Gift taxes and estate taxes have been "merged" into a single tax called the "unified tax."

Grantor – See Settlor

Grantor Trust – An irrevocable grantor trust is drafted so that income tax liability on trust assets is paid by the grantor or creator of the trust. Assets transferred into the trust are no longer part of the Grantor's estate.

Grantor Retained Annuity Trust (GRAT) – An irrevocable trust where the grantor of the trust property (e.g., highly-appreciating stock) receives a fixed income stream during a term of years, and the remaining assets are distributed tax-free or at a discount to the beneficiaries.

Grantor Retained Interest Trust (GRIT) – An irrevocable trust into which you transfer assets, such as a personal residence, closely held business interest, or assets that generate income and are expected to appreciate substantially, while retaining an interest for a period of years. At the end of the period of years, the assets in the trust pass to your beneficiaries, such as a child or grandchild, or to another trust for their benefit.

Gross Estate – The total value of an estate at the date of the decedent's death. The value is determined before debts and other "deductions" are subtracted from the estate value.

Heir – A person entitled to inherit a portion of the estate of a person who has died without a Will.

Inheritance Tax – A tax imposed upon the transfer of property from a deceased person's estate. "Inheritance Tax" is a term which is usually applied to the taxes charged by a state, where as the taxes imposed by the federal government are usually referred to as estate taxes.

Intentionally Defective Irrevocable Trust (IDIT) – An irrevocable trust in which the grantor retains a controlling interest in trust-owned assets. It often offers significant tax advantages.

Inter Vivos Revocable Trust – One name for a living trust. "Inter vivos" is Latin for "between the living."

Irrevocable Life Insurance Trust (ILIT) – A type of irrevocable trust used to hold life insurance. When a life insurance policy is held in an insurance trust, it is protected from estate taxes when the insured dies, provided the trust is established properly, managed properly, and the insured does not retain any "incidents of ownership."

Irrevocable Trust – A trust that cannot be changed, canceled, or "revoked" once it is set up. A "living trust" is not an irrevocable trust. Insurance trusts, GRITs and Dynasty Trusts are examples of irrevocable trusts. Irrevocable trusts are treated by the IRS very differently than revocable trusts.

Insurance Trust – See Irrevocable Life Insurance Trust (ILIT)

Issue – A legal term used in wills and trusts meaning one's children, grandchildren, etc., either through birth or adoption.

Life Estate – The right to have all of the benefit of a property during one's lifetime.

Limited Liability Company (LLC) – A type of business whose owners actively participate in the organization's management and are protected against personal liability for the organization's debts and obligations.

Limited Liability Partnership (LLP) – A type of partnership in which individual partners are protected against personal liability for certain partnership liabilities.

Living Trust – A type of revocable trust used in estate planning to avoid probate, help in situations of incompetency, and allow "smooth" management of assets after the death of the grantor or person who established the trust. The trust can be effective in eliminating or reducing estate taxes for married couples. Revocable Living trusts are established during the life of the grantor, who retains the right to the income and principal and the right to amend or revoke the trust. When the grantor dies, the trust becomes irrevocable and acts as a substitute for a traditional will.

Marital Deduction – The unlimited deduction allowed under federal estate tax law for all qualifying property passing from the estate of the deceased spouse to the surviving spouse. The value of the property passing to the surviving spouse under the marital deduction is "deducted" from the deceased spouse's estate before federal estate taxes are calculated on the estate. Proper planning and use of the deduction allows more property to pass estate tax-free to the family. The Marital Deduction is not available to non-citizens. See QDOT.

Marital Deduction Trust – See Survivor's Trust

Personal Property – Property other than real estate (land and permanent structures on the land). Cars, furniture, securities, bank accounts, and animals are examples of personal property.

Personal Residence Trust (PRT) – A form of a Grantor Retained Interest Trust (GRIT) used to transfer ownership of the residence and capture tax advantages.

Pet Trust – A trust established for the benefit of a pet who survives you. Trust terms provide for the health and well-being of the favored pet.

Portability – This allows surviving spouses to take advantage of estate tax protection that was not properly utilized at the time of the first death. This opportunity is not automatic, in that appropriate steps must be taken at the time of the first death to preserve this option.

Pour-over Will – A will which contains a clause that transfers some or all of the assets that pass through the will into a trust for final distribution from the trust. The will's assets are said to "pour over" into the trust.

Power of Appointment – The power given to a person, by appointment in a will or a trust, to distribute the property that passes through the will or trust at the discretion of the person appointed.

Prenuptial Agreement – A contract between two potential marriage partners specifying how the property owned by each prior to marriage and owned individually or jointly during marriage will be divided should the couple divorce.

Probate – The legal process which facilitates the transfer of a deceased person's property whether they leave a will or die without a will.

Qualified Domestic Trust (QDOT) – A type of trust that allows taxpayers who are not U.S. citizens to maximize for estate tax protections.

Qualified Personal Residence Trust (QPRT) – See Grantor Retained Interest Trust

Reversionary Interest – An interest that a grantor transferred to another person or entity, but which will revert back to the grantor if and when a certain event occurs.

Revocable Trust – A trust which can be amended or revoked by the person(s) who established the trust.

Revocable Living Trust – See Living Trust

Real Property – Land and attachments to the land, such as buildings, fences, etc.

Rule Against Perpetuities (RAP) – A legal rule limiting the duration of a trust's existence. Trust property must be distributed no later than 21 years after the death of the transferor or other designated person.

Settlor - A person who establishes a trust. The term settlor is often used interchangeably with the terms "trustor" and "grantor."

Special Needs Trust (SNT) – A trust for the benefit of a disabled or older person who is receiving government benefits. Assets in such trusts are not counted in determining eligibility.

Stepped-up Basis – The new basis established for a property after the owner's death if the property is in the owner's estate.

Successor Trustee – The trustee who takes over when the initial trustee can no longer function.

Surviving Spouse – The husband or wife that lives after the death of his or her spouse.

Survivor's Trust – A revocable trust that contains the surviving spouse's property interest, over which that spouse has total control. See AB Trust for further explanation.

Taxable Estate – The portion of an estate that is subject to federal or state estate taxes.

Trust – A legal document in which property is held and managed by a trustee for the benefit of another known as a beneficiary. A trust is a relationship in which property is held by one person for the benefit of another.

Trust Corpus or Res – The property of a trust.

Trustee – The person or institution that manages the trust property under the terms of the trust.

Trustor – See Settlor

Unified Credit – A tax credit is given to each person by the IRS to be used during his or her life or after his or her death. The tax credit equals the amount of tax (gift or estate) which is assessed on the exemption equivalent value of property. It is considered the "unified" credit because it applies to both gift taxes and estate taxes and results from the IRS's effort to unify these two taxes or make them consistent.

Valuation Discount – A discount or reduction in the value of an asset for estate valuation purposes. It can be based on a lack of marketability, limited control, loss of control, or the inability to quickly sell the asset at a known price with minimal transaction costs.

Bibliography

1. Gilfix, Michael, with Regan, Morgan, and English, *Tax, Estate, and Financial Planning for the Elderly: Forms and Practice*, Matthew Bender, LEXIS-NEXIS (2012, updated bi-annually).

2. Internal Revenue Code of 1986, as amended.

3. Silverstein, Rachel Emma, *The Wall Street Journal Complete Estate-Planning Guidebook*, Crown Business, 2011.

4. Yablon, Jeffrey, *As Certain As Death: Quotations about Taxes*, Tax Analysts, April 2010.